Interplay

Interplay:
A Theory of Religion and Education

Gabriel Moran

Saint Mary's Press
Christian Brothers Publications
Winona, Minnesota

ISBN: 0-88489-125-9
Library of Congress Catalog Card Number: 80-53203

Contents

Acknowledgments

I wish to thank the following publishers for permission to reprint material originally published by them:

Paulist Press for chapter four, originally published in *The Aesthetic Dimensions of Religious Education,* eds. Gloria Durka and Joanmarie Smith, 1979, pp. 153-164.

W. H. Sadlier for chapter nine, originally published in *Living Light* 16 (Fall 1979), pp. 277-289.

Saint Mary's Press for chapter seven, originally published in *PACE 9* (March, April, May, 1979), and for chapter eleven, originally published in *PACE 10* (October 1979 - February 1980).

Religious Education Association for chapter six, originally published in *Religious Education* 74 (March/April, 1979), pp. 159-172.

1
The Need
for Religious Education

This book is written from the conviction that religious education is one of the most universal, most urgent, and most practical questions confronting our society today. I am also convinced that religious education is still being mishandled even in the church and synagogue, where one might assume it would be of paramount importance. This judgment is not meant to belittle the good and sometimes heroic work of Christian and Jewish educators. But there remains some massive gap in our perception of the very question of religious education.

In criticizing the present I am not looking back nostalgically to some era when everyone could quote the Bible or catechism. The present is by no means the worst of times. In the Boston church of the 1630s Thomas Shepherd was complaining that the congregation "is quite sermonproof nowadays. Are not men blockish, dull, senseless, heavy under all means?"[1] The same complaint, of course, is made by church leaders today. In an institution such as the church there is a tendency to redouble the effort in what could be the wrong cause. Traditional church practices like the sermon may need rethinking in the context of what has happened educationally in the modern world.

I make no assumption that people are more evil and corrupt today. (Nor do I make the opposite assumption that we have evolved beyond the capital sins.) What does differentiate the contemporary world is that each of us is exposed individually to diverse opinions, to an erosion of many traditions, and to pressures that we "make something" out of our lives. Religion plays a powerful part as individuals try to choose their futures and nations try to work out their destinies in a precariously interdependent world. Religion has not disappeared as the men of the eighteenth and nineteenth-century Enlightenment assumed it would. However, those men were not entirely misguided. As many of them recognized, religion can be among the most primitive, blinding, and destructive forces on earth, but there is evidence, too, that religion can be of inestimable value in human life. If religion is to be of this latter quality, then education in religious matters is indispensable.

9

The case for a serious attention to religious education would seem to be obvious. However, what has happened is that the size and complexity of the issue has far outstripped the resources and the tools to deal with it. When a problem becomes overwhelmingly large, human beings have a capacity not to see it. Even in the institutions which are specifically religious, there is actually little attention paid to educational ideas or to the devising of more adequate educational forms. The church and the synagogue assign a minimum of resources to religious education, while the rest of society does not even conceive it to be society's problem.

Like many other people, I have worked for several decades at religious education with limited success. The underlying problem finally dawned upon me; namely, that there does not yet exist any clearly discernible field that can accurately be called *religious education.* My problem was not a lack of success in the field, but the absence of a field to be in. That recognition drastically changes the purpose of a book like this one. My intention is not to tell the reader how to engage in religious education; instead it is something more modest, yet more comprehensive. I ask the reader to take whatever he or she is doing and consider its relation to the theoretical schemes to be presented here. If my ideas and frameworks are persuasive, then I would hope that the practices of the reader will be supported, clarified, and sometimes redirected.

I am trying in this book to set forth a theory of religious education, or at least to contribute to such a theory. I shall especially concentrate upon a consistent language, the prerequisite of a field of study. Protestant churches usually speak of *Christian education;* corresponding activities in the Catholic church are called *catechetics.* These two areas are closely related to religious education but they are not the same thing. A catechetical theory or a theory of Christian education does not constitute a theory of religious education although each of them may fill out part of the meaning of religious education. If a consistent theory is to be stated, one must distinguish terms that logically and historically are not interchangeable.

The description of the term *religious education* is the task of this whole book. What can be said here at the start is that the meaning must comprehend the educational practices of diverse religious groups. We need a language which does justice to both the religious and the educational in life. While the practice of religious groups throughout the centuries is one of our guides, the twentieth century presents us with a genuinely new situation. On the one side is a distinct language of education and a set of institutions to go with it. On the other side we have a religious language, or rather several religious languages, which must inevitably confront the educational language of the modern world. I would suggest that there are three possible outcomes from such a confrontation of religion and education.

In the first case, the religious group adopts the techniques and limited aims of education, but it protects itself against the possibly corrosive effects of rational criticism. For example, if Muslim education begins with the principle that "every child is born a Muslim," then many important educational questions are already answered. In searching for the means to make explicit the natural Islam of the soul, an elaborate theory of Muslim education may be developed. However, such a theory does not constitute a theory of religious education because it cannot transcend Islam.

A second possibility is that education makes the judgments. As education throughout the modern world has grown, especially at the university level, religion often seems overmatched or in actuality never gets a hearing at all. Religion may be allowed into the curriculum as one subject among many, but it is the educator's job to rule upon the acceptability of religious expressions. Thus, the saying in Islam that "every child is born a Muslim" is likely to be dismissed as absurdity or superstition. In this case we have theories of education that may include religion but not a theory of religious education, that is, a theory of learning to live religiously in the modern world.

The third possibility is that we develop a language that would truly deserve the name *religious education.* In this case, the peculiar features of religious language would be respected even as one tries to understand the language. To take the same example once more, "every child is born a Muslim" is neither the answer nor an absurdity. A religious education would have to challenge the truth of the statement, but only as the religious educator tries to see what the Muslim sees. In so doing, a Christian might recognize that Christianity regularly makes a comparable claim, namely, that the soul is "naturally Christian," that children can "grow up Christian, and never know themselves as being otherwise."[2] Can either the Muslim claim or the Christian claim be defended? Can both be correct? A field of religious education would be the place to ask such questions. A field of religious education would therefore have to include (1) a respect for the concrete, particular, and sometimes mysterious practices of the religious life, including what apparently are outrageous claims and (2) an application of the mind with all of its critical capacity for the study, understanding, and teaching of religion.

This meaning of religious education has not received much theorizing. Perhaps that fact should not be surprising if the need for the field has clearly emerged only in the twentieth century. What I shall describe in chapter 2 is the history of what Protestant literature calls "the religious education movement." Although the writers of that period were indeed intent on developing a theory of religious education, it is presumptuous to call this body of writing *the* religious education movement. At most the writers can be seen to have begun to formulate a theory of religious education. The fact that nearly all of the writers were white, male, liberal, and Protestant was a severe limitation to carrying the theory very far. Yet their work should not be dismissed because of biases which are fairly easy to spot today. Neither does it make sense to dismiss all theorizing about religious education simply because the explorations of white, male, liberal Protestants in the early twentieth century have proved inadequate.

Many Catholic and Protestant books talk about religious education, but any consistent language for theorizing is difficult to find. A good recent survey is *Resurgence of Religious Instruction* by Didier-Jacques Piveteau and J. T. Dillon.[3] The authors cover mainly Catholic but also Protestant writings of the past twenty-five years. After surveying the past, they begin their own constructive section by announcing that "the vision of reform has been given clear enough shape by our prophets" and that "from this present day onward the years must see a decline in theoretical studies and an increase in practical applications modest yet concrete."[4] Their announcement, to put it mildly, is premature. Their own book is an all too clear example that there is no consistent language with which to theorize. They often use *catechetics, Christian education,* and *religious instruction* interchangeably with *religious education.* Sometimes there are distinctions implied, but the distinctions are never made clear. Despite the wealth of material contained in this book, I still did not know at the end of the book what topic the book was trying to address.

We cannot develop a field of religious education while speaking of theory as something we have had too much of and something that must be slowly eliminated. Theory, in its original and still operative meaning, is to look carefully at something. To theorize is to penetrate with the mind and to come to some consistent description. Good theory looks at what people are already doing and proposes that there is a better way to describe their activities. The heart of theory is the setting forth of language that is comprehensive, consistent, and precise. For example, a good theory of education should include the family as well as the school. Furthermore, it should distinguish carefully between family activity and school activity. The result might be that a school teacher would do fewer things, would do them better, and would not feel guilty about omitting some things. For their part, the parents of a family might see their work within a larger scheme of meaning, recognizing why they have instinctively been doing some things and why they might wish to change some other practices.

A book which theorizes about religious education has to reflect on what already exists in the religious and educational areas. I am not proposing some new system of ideas which would first have to be accepted on an abstract level and then be applied to practice. The theory in this book is mainly the proposal of some distinctions that would lead to *religious education's* becoming the name of a comprehensive and consistent field of activity. My hope is that the reader might (1) understand better why he or she is doing certain things, (2) decide to describe some of those things in a different way, and (3) recognize more allies in doing what needs doing. For example, in the theorizing on religious education here, a person in "retreat work" has an important part to play. I would hope this book helps people in the church who do retreat work to see new connections to the work of school teachers, parents, and other allies they have inside and outside the church.

I have referred to the need to be rigorously consistent in making certain distinctions. It may be helpful to provide a preview of three of the themes which run throughout the book and the distinctions I insist upon. At the least, the following three distinctions will illustrate the method I pursue. Here at the beginning I am not interested in getting the reader to accept my way of relating the words in these pairs. For now I am only interested in pressing the point that we need consistently to distinguish between the two terms.

(1) **Education and school.** Almost everyone who writes on education would grant that the words *education* and *school* are not synonymous. However, few writers are entirely consistent when it comes to practicing this distinction. I cite one example from a writer who surely wishes to maintain the distinction. Joseph Featherstone, surveying the field of family literature, writes: "Current interest in the family expresses this loss of confidence in education, which in turn reflects the loss of faith in politics and government."[5] What Featherstone presumably means is not a loss of confidence in education but a loss of confidence in the school. People have almost unbounded faith in education, but many wonder if their school is providing a good education. The significance of the school/education distinction is evident here because the school and the family ought to be cooperating in education, but the family obviously cannot do so if education and school are co-extensive in meaning. A large part of the school's problem is the assumption that school is the possessor of education, an assumption Featherstone unwittingly reinforces. A discussion of education would have richer possibilities if we were always to speak of the school as a place for one specific kind of education, and of the family as the provider of another specific part of education.

I have used the family as an illustration of what should not be excluded from education. Exactly how education should be described is a question that is addressed in the chapters that follow. I will refer to *schooling* as one form of education, that is, the specific kind of learning that is most appropriate to the institution of school. In addition, there is a *nonschooling* part of education, that is, a form or several forms of learning that may be found in school but also occur in the context of other institutions. If the distinction between school and education is to be operative we need to name other forms that education takes. My way of naming these forms is open to debate, but the initial step of distinguishing school and education is what I am most interested in here.

If other forms of education besides schooling were clearly and repeatedly named, a great burden would be lifted from the school. In this country schools are asked to do everything and, when they fail, as fail they must, they are periodically attacked by would-be reformers.[6] A *reform* ought to deal with *form*. In educational reform that would mean acknowledging two things about the school: (a) it is indispensably important, and (b) it is limited to one part of education. John Dewey, like many lesser writers on education, could not find the way to affirm both principles together. At the beginning of *Democracy and Education* he wrote: "Schools are, indeed, one important method of transmission which forms the disposition of the immature; but it is only one means, and, compared with other agencies, a relatively superficial means."[7] Here Dewey, while clearly distinguishing school and education, actually underplays the role of the school. More often the effect of Dewey's writing was to overplay the school. By writing despairingly of other agencies, like family and church, Dewey unwittingly turned everything back to "the relatively superficial means" of the school.

At present we seem to be in a swing back to saying that school is important.[8] In the late 1960s and early 1970s many educational reformers had written off the school as beyond reform. Now there is widespread recognition that this strategy leads only to vagueness, or to new schools that are no better than the old ones. The new wave of reform, lest it be nostalgic or reactionary, needs to distinguish between schooling as a form of learning that is still indispensable and other kinds of learning that are important but not necessarily the work of the school. For example, television is an important source of learning today. The school should recognize this fact and exercise a critical role in relation to television. Television can and should be criticized within the school, but television mainly belongs somewhere else than in school. What is disastrous to the school is the assumption that television has made or will make literacy less important. The form of learning I have called *schooling* refers to the acquisition of literacy and the appreciation of literature. Books are an indispensable source of human learning. Books are not the whole of education but they are the central point for the existence of schools.

I would simply note in passing here that religion would especially benefit from the twofold principle: school is indispensably important, and schooling is one limited form of education. Judaism, Christianity, and Islam are indeed, in the Muslim phrase, "religions of the book." Anyone who deprecates the value of schooling does a disservice to these religions and perhaps to all religion. On the other hand, the religious life does not especially flourish in school. Religious education cannot be exclusively the job of school teachers. We should not exclude things like prayer, social action, and family life from the definition of religious education.

(2) **Christian and religious.** Turning from education to the religious we find a distinction that is almost parallel. Practically all writers acknowledge that *Christian* and *religious* are not synonymous. Yet Christian writers regularly slide into a use of language in which the religious is swallowed by the Christian. There are two variations on this swallowing: the main one is to assume that Christianity as the highest form of religion is the only one worth talking about in our society. A subsidiary move is to acknowledge that religions exist but to assert that true Christianity is above mere religion. In the first case no distinction is allowed; in the second case there is separation rather than distinction. In both cases the religious disappears—a move that is illogical and self-defeating.

The reason for *Christian* replacing *religious* is parallel to *school's* taking over *education*; that is, any other way of speaking seems to drift into vagueness. The distinction between Christian and religious is even more difficult to make for two reasons: first, religion (more than education) is hotly particular—no religious devotee accepts the possibility of being generally religious. Second, and connected to the first, no one can propose an adequate model or typology for all the forms of religious life. If Christian is one form, what are the names of the others? It is possible to list those three, five, or ten names that are somewhat comparable to *Christian,* but is that in any sense a typology of forms? Is *Christian* itself a form of religious life or must we not specify Lutheran Christian or Orthodox Christian? There are many schemes for classifying religious forms (for example, those with a personal god and those with a nonpersonal absolute). Some of them can be useful distinctions, but the world is nowhere near having any system that categorizes religions in a clear, comprehensive, and unbiased way.

Despite this insuperable problem of religious categories, it is nonetheless possible and desirable to distinguish *Christian* and *religious.* The same twofold principle used in reference to schooling applies here: (a) Christian is indispensably important (at least for those who live by it) as one form or several forms of the religious life; (b) Christian is only one form or several forms among the many; even for its own health today it needs the complementarity of other forms. If one were a Buddhist or Muslim, that twofold principle would be reworded, but the principle of distinction would be the same.

Chapter 3 of this book confronts directly the claim to specialness or "uniqueness" on the part of a religion. Chapter 4 investigates this question through the category I find most helpful, namely, revelation. In both chapters I make the claim that we can affirm the particular without abandoning the universal, that in fact the universal can only be affirmed in and through the most concrete and particular forms of religious life. If that principle is correct, then one can be entirely devoted to one specific form of religious life without being arrogant, narrow-minded, or intolerant of others.

Throughout these essays and especially in chapter 7, I refer to concrete examples. I usually choose Christian ones and less frequently some that are Jewish. That choice simply reflects the limits of my personal experience. In religious matters every one of us works within a very limited range of experience. The range today may be greater than ever before, but it is still limited in each individual's life. Nonetheless, every person today has the duty to distinguish between the religious and one form of religiousness, such as Christian. One doesn't need a Ph.D. in religion to recognize that the distinction is valid, important, and necessary.

(3) **Religious education and Christian education.** This distinction obviously follows from the two that have preceded. By no stretch of logic can the terms *Christian education* and *religious education* be made synonymous. Once again lip service is paid to a distinction between the two, but in practice the distinction is not regularly observed. The reasoning seems to be the same as in the two previous distinctions, namely, that Christian education is the name for the only real religious education there is, that Christian education is the concrete and particular form religious education must have lest it disappear into the clouds.

The most interesting case to bring up in challenging this usage is education within Judaism. I would think it obvious that collapsing the difference between religious and Christian education eliminates Jewish concerns and could easily be taken as an insult by Jews. I am amazed at the continuing insensitivity of Christian writers and speakers on this point. I have been at scores of religious education meetings which included Jews and Christians where the terms *religious education* and *Christian education* were used interchangeably.

Jews have their own aggressive form of particularism when it comes to religious education. They would hardly ever claim that Jewish education and religious education are identical, but their concentration upon transmitting the Jewish religion may severely limit their interest in any other meaning of religious education. Jews are understandably concerned with preserving Judaism in a country that is 97 percent non-Jewish. For Jews to raise the question of religious education, and not only the question of Jewish education, involves a degree of risk. But Judaism even more than Christianity would benefit from an increased understanding of religion throughout the whole population. Furthermore, a religion can be "transmitted" today only in the context of a continuing conversation with other religions.

An interesting facet of the term *Christian education* is that it nearly always excludes Roman Catholics. Lodged in the term are the 370 years of usage on these shores that makes Protestant and Christian interchangeable. That usage has been slowly changing in recent decades but not in the term *Christian education*. When a list of writers on Christian education is given, the list will invariably include only Protestants. This peculiarly intolerant language in an area which is called educational deserves extensive examination. The problem is not eliminated by a promise to let some Catholics in. There is need for a context of religious education in which Catholics, Protestants, Jews, and others can converse about educational matters.

Catholic writers in the United States generally adopt a language that developed in the European church. Catholics have a language that reflects among other things the Bible, church councils, sacramental spirituality, medieval scholasticism, and modern theology. Catholics in this country modify the language to a degree, but the internal language of the Roman Catholic church has a remarkably consistent character throughout the world. That situation is not a bad one; in fact it has great advantages both in administrative matters and in sacramental participation.

The place where this uniformity of language becomes questionable is in education. Even here there is a valid part of education in which Catholics ask the best way to pass on Catholicism. But, as I said of Judaism, it may be beneficial to Catholicism's survival and enrichment to ask also about a wider meaning of religious education. Whatever that question means, it cannot even be asked if the current language of Roman Catholicism is assumed to be the only possible language of religious education. Catholics collapse the distinction through the word *catechetics*, a term that has become popular in the last two decades. *Catechist, catechize, catechesis* (and the better known word *catechism*) are ancient terms with rich connotations, but the words hardly exist today outside the Catholic church.[9]

The Catholic church has the right and possibly the duty to preserve this language of catechetics. What would be illogical and unwise is to collapse the difference between catechetics and religious education. In a move that parallels the Protestant use of "Christian education," Catholic writers often assume that catechetics is the only concrete and existing form of religious education. In an article which ironically enough appears in *Religious Education,* Wilfred Paradis writes: "If *Sharing the Light of Faith* has its expected impact, the words religious education will practically disappear to be replaced by catechetics and catechesis. Religious education will be used to signify transmitting information . . ."[10] Paradis' desire here to support the National Catechetical Directory is laudable, but advocating the practical disappearance of the term *religious education* is unnecessary and self-defeating. The final comment on retaining the term for "transmitting information" further confuses the issue.

In summary, my insistence on the distinction between religious education and Christian education points most directly at the Protestant offender. I have also indicated that a similar tendency could be found for Jewish, Catholic, Orthodox, and Muslim writers. What they are trying to defend may need defending; what they are trying to transmit may be worth passing on. However, in affirming what they know as good, they may imply the denial of something else which is good and even necessary today. The first six chapters of this book try to describe a field of religious education as the context for Jewish, Protestant, Muslim, and other religious bodies engaging in their own forms of education. Chapter 7 switches from consideration of an academic field to consideration of a profession. I examine the relation of a proposed or existing profession of religious education and the profession of Christian church minister. Therein I claim the need for two consistent and complementary languages, one the language of church ministry and the other the language of modern education.

My overall intention is to develop a field/profession of religious education that is not reducible to church definitions. This project strikes some people as misguided and dangerous. Undoubtedly it does open the church doors to powerful and dangerous forces. The churches have been generally suspicious of educational philosophies from the eighteenth century to the present. The push of modern education has often seemed to be in the direction of edging God out of the world and corroding ancient traditions. Church strategy has often been simply to stand against the tide although a minority of church members ride with the tide. The three distinctions which I have proposed would allow for a third possibility, namely, a genuine appreciation of modern education but a refusal to allow the last word to modern secularisms.

Education, in this context, would have the benefit of serious challenges by specific religious forms. One of the deficiencies of modern education followed from its acceptance of the Christian claim that the religious is reducible to given ecclesiastical forms. Modern education has a responsibility to rediscover the wide and deep meaning of *religious.* Education, as it is often rationalistically conceived, may be an enemy of religious life. One way to change that picture is to bring the concerns of religion within the educational framework. Education becomes more true to itself if it does not exclude religious concerns.

I hope that my last four chapters demonstrate this point. In chapter 8, I am very critical of "adult education" both in its history and in its current form. Adult education assumes that religion belongs in churches and synagogues. By introducing religious issues into the general question of adult education, I propose to transform the very meaning of adult education. A related issue in chapters 9 and 10 is the study of development in children's and adults' lives. I propose in chapter 9 that schemes of moral development are radically changed if one admits religion into the discussion. In chapter 10, I question schemes of adult development that are scandalously deficient in their treatment of religion, using as my example the fact that one cannot understand the middle-aged male in this country without asking religious questions.

The final chapter of the book takes me back to my opening statement. Religious education is of urgent and practical necessity in an unjust world. I am concerned in this chapter with understanding religious education in such a way that the movement for social justice is the center of the process rather than a peripheral bit of content. All education purports to deal with justice; a religious education questions whether we know what justice means and whether we are certain of how to get there. I try to end not with paralyzing questions but with definite steps that can realistically be taken. We do not know the full meaning of God's justice, and none of us knows how to make a just world. But we should be able to recognize injustice and to take steps that reduce the world's sorrows. Religious education is not a panacea, but it can be a significant help toward walking humbly and justly on God's earth.

2
The Limits
of the Past

Is religious education an idea whose time has passed? The answer to that question depends upon the meaning of the term *religious education.* With the meaning that is assumed in most of U.S. Protestantism the answer is "Yes. Religious education was an idea, an ideal, and a movement that was tried and found wanting. Religious education came to an end in the 1940s, and since then Protestant seminaries and congregations have returned to their genuine mission of 'Christian education.' "

Many Catholics and Jews are unfamiliar with the meaning of *religious education* as referred to in Protestant literature. For them the term does not designate an historical movement. What Protestants call "the religious education movement" was inherently weak in being almost exclusively Protestant. As I indicate below, that was not the intent of the movement nor its original design, but that is the way it turned out. If religious education was tried only by Protestantism—in its liberal wing—can we assume that the religious possibilities of education and the educational needs of religion have been thoroughly explored?

Catholics, Jews, and other groups do occasionally use the term *religious education* but usually as a secondary term for "passing on the faith" within each tradition. Jews find the term useful in any dialogue with Christian educators. Catholics probably use the term more than anybody else because the term *Catholic education* still usually refers to the Catholic school system. Thus, the educating of Catholics outside those schools is frequently called *religious education.* In no religious body is the term *religious education* used with much determination and great enthusiasm. It seems to be a project with an undistinguished past and a doubtful future.

The theme of this book is that religious education, far from being an idea that has passed, is an idea whose time has not yet arrived. Up to now the human race has gotten along without a developed system of religious education, but the advent of a single world history in the second half of the twentieth century is shaking loose the world's parochialisms. If a few religious fanatics can seize a plane (or an atomic bomb) and paralyze world affairs, the need to examine and understand religion becomes clearer. If ferment within Islam changes the price of heating oil for all our homes, we may finally recognize that the education of Muslims and a Christian understanding of Islam are important issues. If religious charlatans can attract followings from the sophisticated suburbs of the United States, there must be some deficiency in the religious understanding provided for our youth.

Religious education as a developed field of activity needs a consistent and comprehensive language. My intention is to propose a framework that would allow for conversation between (1) Jewish, Catholic, Orthodox, Protestant, Muslim, and other groups; (2) religious educators and other educators; (3) religious institutions and public institutions of learning. The natural tendency here is to abstract from all the differences between religions. Down that path lie generalities and abstractions which cannot get at the real questions of religious life. The better route is to take whatever religious language we know and carefully examine it in relation to educational institutions and to other religious possibilities.

The religious education movement, as we shall see in the next section, tried to move quickly toward a unified language of religious education. However, the movement could not even succeed in reaching interdenominational Protestant agreement. But the point of religious education, as I shall propose, is not to reach a high level of abstraction that subsumes religions as individual cases; it is to reach an understanding of the religious lives of people. At the end of this chapter, then, I shall propose imagery which offers a greater range of possibilities for exploring both the intramural worlds of Christianity, Judaism, and Islam and the relationships between those differing religious worlds.

But first it will be useful to consider the history and context of the religious education movement and their implications. The movement was fatally flawed from the beginning, but its leaders were grasping at something important. Today's educators still have something to learn from the period.

The Movement

A convenient way to get a view of this history might be through the collection *Who Are We? The Quest for a Religious Education*.[1] The editor, John Westerhoff, culled the articles from the journal *Religious Education* on the seventy-fifth anniversary of the Religious Education Association. While in the judgment of many people the movement itself ended about 1940, the Association has continued. One could consider its continued existence an anachronism, but I would prefer to think of the

REA as a kind of U.N. flag. It has not the power or prestige to bring about religious education, but it has remained a forum for those few or many who think that the future requires religious education.

The beginning of the movement is usually dated from the founding of the Association in 1903. An impressive cross-section of four hundred delegates came to the first meeting. They included university presidents, administrators, and public school teachers. A number of Catholics and Jews accompanied the Protestant representation. The purpose of the meeting was admirably stated as: "To inspire the educational forces of our country with the religious ideal; to inspire the religious forces of our country with the educational ideal."[2] I would think that this purpose is even more important in the last two decades of the twentieth century than it was in the first decade.

Some people would probably say that for the REA it was all downhill after the first meeting. Nearly everyone would agree that the Association has never fulfilled its idealistic hopes. I think we have a duty in any case to try to pinpoint the movement's specific strengths and weaknesses. In particular, we have to ask whether it was the ideal that was wrong or whether there was a deficiency in the means available. If the latter was the case, then the need today is to redesign the means and to reinitiate the movement from wherever history has left it.

As a start, I would suggest a distinction that occurred to me in reading *Who Are We?* The search for a religious education was a search for two different things: (1) an academic field or discipline, (2) a profession. The two things are closely related but they are not reducible to the same question. Nearly all of the essays in that volume are much more concerned with a prospective field than a profession.

Probably in all cases, but certainly in this one, it is easier to invent a field than a profession. The existence of an academic field would be a necessary but not a sufficient condition of the profession. Moreover, the construction of an academic field is a relatively easy affair. A group of people gather some ideas under a unifying method. If the material can be fitted into the departmental structure of a university, it may get recognition as an academic discipline.

Profession is an ambiguous term that I will investigate later. But in the contemporary world it involves a starkly realistic question: Who pays whom to do what? Professions have emerged because there was a market—people who needed (or thought they needed) a service. A new profession requires not only a specialized knowledge but also institutional changes arranged by the government or some powerful agency. A new profession needs the support of institutions that deliver services as well as acceptance by some public that financially values what is offered.

The distinction between field and profession would make clearer the shift that occurred around the year 1940, a shift always noted in histories of religious education. The usual way of describing the shift is to say that liberal theology was replaced by conservative theology. If one thinks of religion only as ideas, that is, as a field of study, then this description of the change seems plausible. Religious education whose content had been a set of liberal religious ideas was reformed by the introduction of a conservative theology. It would be thought that, for reasons not entirely clear, the term *Christian education* came to replace *religious education* as the most common way to refer to this field of study.

When one looks at this shift from the standpoint of a profession, the change is much more drastic. The hope in the early part of the century had been to create not just an academic field of religious education but a new profession. Individuals and groups tried to establish standards for "the professional religious educator." The profession of religious education was to be part of a larger movement to put all education on a professional footing. Each Protestant church was envisioned as having a professional educator. The hope for a new profession met with varying degrees of success through the first four decades of the century. In the 1940s the movement came to a halt. The change from religious education to Christian education was not the reform of a profession but the end of a hoped-for profession and the beginning or reestablishing of a (sub)profession. *Christian education* became the name for a professional role within the church's own profession, the profession which Protestants have always called *ministry.*

The change from liberal to conservative theology, therefore, is at most a symptom of what happened. It was less a case of the church going conservative in theology than a case of the church recovering control of its education. Success in bringing everything back under the aegis of church ministry can be viewed as a progressive move. Educational programs may be better organized within Christian education, and they almost certainly become more substantial in doctrinal and scriptural ways. But candor and clarity are needed here lest the move from religious education to Christian education preempt other possibilities.

The failure to admit that one profession stopped and another took over is what allows Protestants frequently to interchange *religious education* and *Christian education.* The assumption seems to be that the latter is simply more concrete and practical. When one objects to this illogical use of terms the point is usually granted but "we know what we mean whatever the name." It is as if baseball and football were thought to have the same aims and means because they are both ball games. Or as a more pertinent example, it is as if someone were to say: "Up to the 1940s there was great hope for democracy but then we became realistic and saw we are the only democracy. From then on Americanism replaced democracy, but it is also all right to use democracy and Americanism interchangeably." Even if it were true that the United States were the only effectively operating democracy, it would be intolerably chauvinistic to conflate the terms *democracy* and *Americanism.* Among other things it would blind us to the difference between the nation of the United States and the dream or myth of America.[3]

Although the religious education profession effectively ceased, some of the factors that brought about the movement still exist. For example, in some parts of the country the Sunday School maintains its distance from the profession of church minister. The relative autonomy of the Sunday School movement has been both a strength and a weakness during its two centuries of existence. The religious education movement began out of dissatisfaction with the Sunday School, but like most reactions it was predicated upon one of the characteristics of its opponent, namely, the independence possessed by the Sunday School. The liberal educators of 1900 to 1940 have had their day, but the Sunday School is still here. If it can adopt some of the positive aspects of modern professionalization, the Sunday School is one base for constructing a future religious education.

Another base for the field/profession of religious education exists today in the Roman Catholic church. The sudden closing of many Catholic schools in the 1960s released a group of people who already thought of themselves as "professional educators" not directly under the control of the clergy. This group formed a nucleus for the attempted invention of the professional religious educator. Many people who have gone this route find that to invent a title (coordinator or DRE) is not to invent a profession. Unless they get more institutional help, the Catholic parish directors of religious education cannot carry out their intention to become a profession.

What seems likely to occur is that the Protestant pattern will be repeated in Catholicism, that is, the hoped for profession of religious education will give way to education's becoming an official part of church ministry. As in the Protestant pattern, one should note both the gain and the loss in this process. The organizational structure becomes neater, and the educational offerings are clearly in line with the official positions of the church. What are eliminated are educational offerings that have some support from the church but are independent of its officials.

By the end of the 1970s the process seemed well advanced. University and seminary degrees are often difficult to distinguish. Some Catholic universities offer courses in religion as distinct from ministerial activities, but millions of Catholics have no connection with the university. In chapter 7, I describe two professions within the education of the Catholic

Christian church. My contention is that every parishioner ought to have the benefit of educators who deal in Catholic church matters as well as ministers of the Catholic church who deal in educational matters.

The Religious and Educational Context of the Movement

A sketch of the period before 1940 will indicate the strengths and weaknesses which are still important for today's rethinking of these issues. First, some comments can be made on the emergence of modern education itself, its high hopes, and its present chastened outlook. Second, there is the issue of what *religious* meant in the early part of this century. Third, the alliance of these notions of *religious* and *education* brought on a reaction in the 1940s, the limitations of which need to be assessed.

1. EDUCATION

What Dewey was calling the "new education" in the 1890s seemed to fit well with the new liberal theology of the time. This agreement should not be too surprising. Both emerged out of the same cultural setting. Education in the schools took over some of the ideas and functions of religion. The schools could find kinship with theology provided that theology did not stress divisive doctrines. Educators stood to profit from the added motivation and quality that the word *religious* implied. The religious enthusiasts saw this union as a step toward final victory. G. A. Coe declared in 1903: "Religious education is not a part of general education, it *is* general education. It is the whole of which our so-called secular education is only a part or a phase."[4]

What kind of thing was being talked about as education in this period? The word that constantly recurs in the literature is *science,* followed by other key phrases: *social, democratic, child-centered, life situations.* In the latter part of the twentieth century both science and education have lost some of their glamor. Science is looked upon with considerable misgivings because of its association with destructive aspects of modern technology. To this day hardly anyone attacks education, but its bright image has been tarnished. We have difficulty today realizing the extraordinary expectations once associated with education. Looking back on the late nineteenth-century movement for suffrage, common schools, and the press, Henry Adams wrote: "On these points doubt was forbidden. Education was divine, and man needed only a current knowledge of facts to reach perfection."[5]

The great trust in science was merely the full flowering of the eighteenth-century trust in reason. Thomas Jefferson, by no means an irreligious man, could optimistically say that we had given an example to the world by founding a government on reason alone. For Tom Paine as for Voltaire, the struggle in the world was between reason and superstition. And the early feminist, Mary Wollstonecraft, could write in 1792: "Children cannot be taught too early to submit to reason, for to submit to reason is to submit to the nature of things, and to that God who formed them so, to promote their real interest."[6] The nineteenth-century successes of science and technology confirmed this trust in reason. Education in the early twentieth century could aspire to no higher ideal than the scientific use of reason. A writer in *Religious Education* could say: "In the light of the experience of the last generation, it is foolhardy to venture to set limits beyond which science cannot go."[7]

Two strategies followed immediately from this exaltation of scientific reason: (1) that the environment should be changed to suit the humans, not vice versa, (2) that the future rather than the past carries weight in practical decisions. The world was thought to be undergoing an acceleration in change. If change could be dominated by men of power, then change was desirable and that is where education came in. "Education in a democracy . . . should be such as to convince everybody that things can be controlled and moulded by the power of man."[8]

Writers on education were impressed by all the new possibilities which seemed to be opening up. The field of psychology led the way in revealing the mysteries of learning and control. Once enough tests had been run, we would know how children learn and how to construct environments where all would learn. The right experiences could be correlated with the child's developing powers so that the child could become a person of power. Other viewpoints from the past were dismissed as outdated. Contrasting experience and knowledge, William C. Bower wrote: "To have a curriculum of knowledge would make education consist in adjustment to the inheritance of the race. But this is precisely what education ought not to be."[9]

The image of time that is implied here is a straight arrow of progress. The past is the points that have disappeared to the left, the future is the set of points to the right of the present and disappearing moment. A famous question of Coe's was "whether the primary purpose of Christian education is to hand on a religion or to create a new world?"[10] The word *primary* saves the question from being a complete dichotomy, that is, one could primarily create a new world in the very act of (secondarily) passing on a religion. Earlier in the same book Coe contrasted the teacher's task as "transmission of the past" or "response to the present." That question is less presumptuous and could be indicative of a different image of time. "Responding to the present" does not have to assume that the future is pitted against the past. But it is difficult to see "response to the present" as an operational description if the present is merely a point between past and future.[11]

The center of education was the child, or more precisely, the "life situations" and unfolding powers of the child. Children would be socialized into democratic society, that is, rational knowledge and technical skill would gradually eliminate the conflicts between humans. The human capacity "to put nature to the rack" would provide an abundance of goods. Coe emphasized that "life situations" was a concept that could be taken superficially. The teacher was supposed to *discriminate* among the child's powers and tendencies.[12] However, Coe and the other religious educators generally sided with the optimistic outlook of science that characterized education in the early decades of this century.

2. LIBERAL RELIGION

Despite Coe's claim that secular education was now subsumed under religious education, the opposite tendency seemed to characterize the religious education movement. All education's becoming religious might be alternately described as education's absorbing any distinctive or particular meaning for the word *religious*. The nineteenth century had seen the passing of a strong patriarchal religion in which God saves man from sin and damnation. But because the male had been in charge of creation in the patriarchal picture, the passing of the all-powerful God did not alter the picture as much as one might have expected. The distinctive patriarchal religion was not followed by a distinct form of matriarchal religion or nature mysticism. Instead, the man who had felt sinful now felt innocent and in charge of his own religious life. George Santayana wrote in 1911: "If you told the modern American that he is totally depraved, he would think you are joking. . . . He is convinced that he always has been, and always will be, victorious and blameless."[13]

As the harsh-sounding Calvinism fell away, the Christian Bible seemed to supply moral inspiration for living in the modern age. There would be a new religion "which will be the fine flower of the modern spirit's achievement."[14] The language was still biblical, or at least there was frequent reference to the life and sayings of Jesus. Surprisingly, the image of "kingdom of God" played a key role in the religious discussion. The image hardly seems compatible with the political aspirations of the time and indeed Coe did try to speak of the "democracy of God." But "kingdom" with its long history in Protestantism remained a powerful image throughout the period.

This image did not connote the same thing in all writers. At times there is little distinction between "kingdom of God" and self-realization. One can hear echoes to this day in self-help books that declare "the kingdom is in us; we already have the key."[15] More often the phrase was linked to the realization of social and political goals. F. Ernest Johnson, writing at the end of the period and trying to salvage the liberal notion, described the kingdom of God "as a project within the historical process which is motivated by a reference to a goal never reached but always envisaged." This developmental, as opposed to eschatological, conception "means only that the orderly process is more normative than the catastrophic."[16] The result, nevertheless, seemed to be an awkward combination of modern science and biblical phrases. No matter how great the insistence on biblical phrases, the process of modern education always seemed to be on the verge of swallowing the religious sentiments.

John Dewey in his 1908 essay "Religion and Our Schools" set up a challenge to all "dogmatic faiths." They are (1) intellectually secret, not public; (2) peculiarly revealed, not generally known; (3) authoritatively declared, not tested in ordinary ways. Dewey believed that there could be no genuine religious education until religions adopted the second position in each of those pairings.[17] The liberal religious movement tried to go in that direction. Religion would be public, generally known, and tested in ordinary ways. One of Dewey's protegés in the religious education movement could dismiss the concepts of supernatural and revelation and by implication most of the religious past: "If experience teaches us that we live in a universe where there is unity, the basic truths of religion must be discoverable in the observable facts of life."[18]

Religion's chief value seemed to be "social"; all of education was concerned with living together in democratic society. Religion was functional in providing rules, inspiration, and insight for people's getting along with one another. It was difficult to criticize a social approach to religion; certainly no one wished to be labeled unsocial. Nonetheless, a recognition of something lacking existed among people who were by no means reactionary. One writer in the 1930s who appreciated the social emphasis nevertheless complained that the cosmic and metaphysical elements had been dismissed as mere by-products. What had been central to most religions—an attitude toward the universe as a whole—was being casually downplayed in the name of the social.[19] That criticism signaled problems for the religious education movement, which seemed to be a social success but was about to become a theological outcast.

3. RELIGIOUS REACTION

When one moves from chapter 7 to chapter 8 of *Who Are We?*, one finds a nearly complete reversal of attitude. Nevin Harner's "Is Religious Education to Become a Science?" contains the elements described above. In contrast, H. Shelton Smith's article, "Let Religious Educators Reckon with the Barthians," is advance warning of the shock that was arriving from Europe. Smith does not represent himself here as a Barthian, but he is sufficiently attracted to the position to be able to formulate its criticisms. The attack may have been more effective because it was performed with critical distance and not polemical fervor. Smith followed up his article with the book *Faith and Nurture,* which is generally credited with having "laid bare ruthlessly the theological assumptions that were practically universal in the movement."[20]

The change within Protestant theology and its delayed impact on religious education was a resistance to erosion within Protestant churches. That there had been an erosion of doctrinal substance can hardly be doubted. It can also be plausibly argued that neo-orthodoxy, a movement usually associated with the name of Karl Barth, was successful. The "Word of God" as found in Christ and Scripture was put back at the center of theology. God was in Christ reconciling the world to himself and only through faith could man be saved.

The reaffirmation of central Christian doctrines may have been what the times demanded. For Barth in Nazi Germany the choice was clear and urgent. Nevertheless, the limited context of the reaction should not be overlooked. The language and the imagery of the proposed alternative were themselves severely limited. Barth's works still influence Christian theology today, but they have undergone extensive criticism in a new ecumenical era. In contrast, the Barthian orthodoxy seemed to stop the religious education movement dead in its tracks, and it has never recovered. H. Shelton Smith's criticism is still with us as definitive evidence that religious education was a misguided venture. In an era when an ecumenically based religious education is urgently needed, the very idea of religious education is widely assumed to be a discredited category.

What was the devastating critique that H. Shelton Smith brought to the religious education movement? As happens in much effective criticism, Smith set up a series of contrasts. Having made the choices evident, he hardly even needed to advocate that one set of choices was woefully inadequate.[21] What resulted from the discrediting of the liberal position was a reassertion of God, Christ, Bible, Sin, Redemption, Conversion, Faith, and all the traditional doctrines of theology. What was lost was the possible exploration of the many forms of religiousness in the modern world. A key weakness of the religious education movement had been its failure to examine the intricate relation of the religious and the Christian, that is, *religious* tended to mean "liberally Christian." The neo-orthodox reaction perpetuated and solidified this failure; it too failed to explore the relation of religious and Christian because the religious was not worth exploring when the Christian answers were already given.

Smith set out a series of choices that confronted theology. The categories in Column A are descriptions of liberal theology, and Column B represents the alternative positions from Smith's point of view.

Column A	Column B
1. Gradual growth (continuity)	1. Revolution (discontinuity)
2. God within	2. God above
3. Self-emancipative reason	3. Faith
4. Anthropocentric	4. Theocentric

I will comment briefly on each of these four oppositions and then I will present a Column C. That is, I wish to claim that the route which was taken forty years ago is not the only alternative to the liberal theology of Column A.

1) The first contrast is between liberalism's view that the kingdom of God could be brought about by human effort and neo-orthodoxy's insistence on the need for divine intervention. At the personal level that meant a choice between the naturally good man and the sinner who needs conversion.

2) The second contast is between a liberal God who is comfortably within human reach and the neo-orthodox God who is above the heavens. Theology often speaks of the immanence of God as over against a transcendent God.

3) Smith describes the project of liberal theology as emancipation through reason alone. To neo-orthodox theology it was clear that faith alone can bring salvation.

4) The final contrast is between a religion that is centered on man and a religion that is centered on God. The neo-orthodox theology reasserted the traditional formula: It is God who saves, not man; it is faith that reveals the final truth, not human reason.

I would like to propose that in each case it is possible to correct the weakness of liberal theology by a route other than the reassertion of the traditional formulas. The third image I provide is compatible with Christian doctrine but it provides more room for imagination and exploration. Such a broadening of possibilities is essential to a religious education that would respect ancient doctrine but challenge its meaning. Christian doctrine needs rethinking in the context of imagery that allows conversation across religious lines. In each case, the first diagram is the liberal position, the second is the neo-orthodox, and the third is my own suggestion for a richer language and imagery.

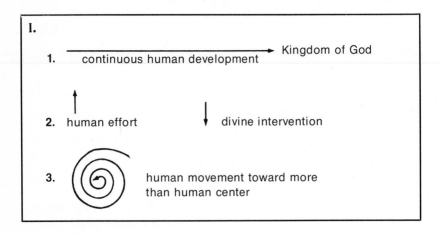

The gradual and continuous growth into the kingdom of God was a premise that no church could long abide. Nonetheless, an intervention of God may not be the best way to describe the relation of divine activity and human history. If both the mysteries of religion and the integrity of education are to be preserved, we need an imagery that does not simplistically force a choice between continuity and discontinuity. In the third image, the kingdom of God arrives with human effort but not as a result of a straight line of human progress.

The first diagram suggests that there is no need for conversion from sin, the second diagram usually means that there is one dramatic conversion. Both Horace Bushnell and George A. Coe accepted the idea of conversion but not in the form indicated by the second image. They both sensed that the second image does not really deserve the name *conversion*, "to turn round." Bushnell's advocacy of education *in conversion* rather than education *for conversion* is suggested by my third diagram. Here the idea of conversion is taken seriously and placed at the center of education. The individual has no gaps of discontinuity, but neither is progress a predictable and straightforward movement. God does not suddenly enter the picture after years of apparent absence. God is the precondition, the end, and the abiding presence in the third image. Each person is called to unexpected ways by other humans and nonhumans who share in the journey.

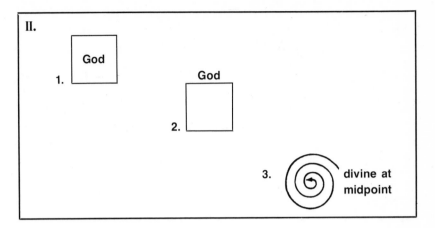

God within or God above appears to offer a clear choice, but every religious tradition warns against the dangers of spatial imagery. The most high God in Judaism is at the same time the God among his people. God may be above all finite things in Islam, but he is also "closer than the great vein in your neck." The religious education movement spoke of God being within. If neo-orthodoxy in reaction said that God is above, that description may be a slight improvement but, taken literalistically, it is every bit as misleading. Religiously one can say that God is to the left and to the right, God is up and down, God is in front and behind. Instead of having to choose between a God within and a God above, we need to use spatial imagery in a way that opens imagination not closes it.

In the third diagram, the word *God* does not appear, but God is "located" at the center of a sphere. God is in all directions from the human but is never under human control. The religious education movement and the neo-orthodox reaction could have been helped by an acquaintance with religious symbolism both Eastern and Western. No image is more frequent in the history of religions than the "centrality" of God. The neo-orthodox reassertion that "God is above" is not rich enough even in relation to Christian symbolism.

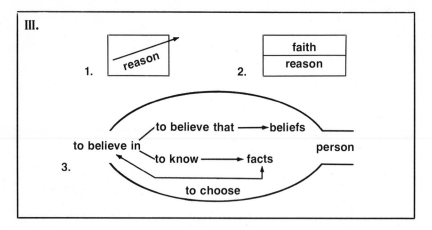

In a contrast between self-emancipative reason on one side and faith on the other, the adjective "self-emancipative" makes reason unaccept-able as a religious choice. But it is not enough today to place faith over reason. We live in a world where human reason has been let loose and cannot be returned to a premodern position. However, faith has not disappeared as the eighteenth century expected it would. The diagram distinguishes three different meanings for the word *faith*. "To believe in," that is, *faith* meaning trust and openness, is widely recognized as indis-pensable to human life. "To believe that," that is, *faith* meaning to hold as true, is an unavoidable necessity for much of what we know. Finally there are beliefs, the object of the verb "to believe that."

The third image describes the meaning of faith as a human quality. Faith (as believing in) is not directed at beliefs but at reality. Each religious group intends to express *the faith,* but each religion falls short of its ambition. When reason is situated where it is in the third diagram, it is not self-emancipative but neither are any arbitrary restrictions placed upon it. No power is above reason in human life, and yet reason remains a very limited instrument whose "factual truth" is usually no better than a well-founded belief. No religious group can put its ultimate trust in reason, but a religion today needs the critical function that reason offers. Reason helps us to determine if our beliefs are becoming more adequate to our faith.

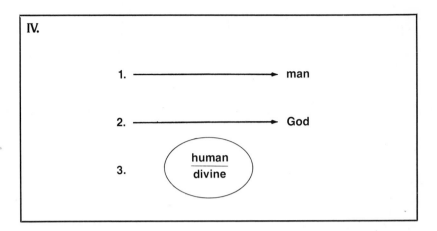

In the last contrast which Smith used, the liberal was accused of being anthropocentric while the reaction claimed to be theocentric. I would claim that, in each of the four cases above, the first and second images are neither theocentric nor anthropocentric. Only the third image can be called -*centric* because it alone has a center. Furthermore, the third is centered on the divine to the extent it is centered on the human. In the Jewish and Christian scheme of creation the human is placed at the center of creation. Modern secularisms have attempted to place human beings *at the top* of everything, which is an entirely different image.

The call to the humility of creatureliness is a call back to the center of creation. A religion of "social relations" does not have a rich enough scope for exploring the relation of humans to all that surrounds them. The full interplay of men and men, men and women, women and women, adults and children, humans and animals, animals and animals, humans and plants, the living and the nonliving, is the matrix of relationships open to God. The choice is between man on the top or the human in the middle. The first is likely to imagine God as a superman; the second leaves open the mysteries of God and creation by expanding the imagery available to represent God.

Conclusion

My intention has been not to ridicule the reaction that brought down the religious education movement but to point out that the issues are not closed. The religious education movement of 1900 to 1940 was deficient in religious imagery and language. The substitution of a Christian education for a religious education was an understandable reaction in the context, but the context has changed. In the 1950s a field of Christian education was developed in close relation to the profession of church ministry. I am suggesting not an attack upon that work but a recognition that the times demand a reexamination of the possibility of a field and a profession of religious education.

My reference to what the times demand is not just to what "modern education" or "contemporary science" claims. I refer also to the searchings and the upheavals within the major religions themselves. Christian and Jewish reforms need an educational context and educational means. Catholic, Protestant, Jewish, and Muslim powers are going to confront each other on the world stage. If education is not a part of what is going on between these groups, one can be assured that violence certainly will be a part. The task of constructing a religious education for the future, far from being a vague, boring, and trivial recasting of tired ideas, is a frighteningly large venture. The ideas and words are not at hand; they have to be patiently discovered, refashioned, or invented. To aid in this effort, in the next chapter I will look at religious education as a field of study and, in chapter 7, I will examine religious education as a profession.

3
Toward a Field
of Religious Education

The immediate problem one confronts in trying to describe a field of religious education is the choice of an approach. The approaches to formulating a description of the field seem to be only two and both seem doomed. One can begin by saying that the question is fundamentally religious; given the nature of religion, what kind of education is appropriate? Alternatively, one can presume that the question falls within education. Knowing the nature of education, where does one fit religion into it?

The first approach is generally what occurs in Protestant, Jewish, and Catholic congregations. Protestants set up Sunday Schools, Catholics run catechetical programs, and Jews give synagogue or temple instruction. While each of these operations may have value, they do not provide the basic elements for a field of religious education. Communication among these three programs is minimal and the relation between these religious operations and public educational institutions is almost nonexistent. So long as they operate in their isolated worlds, Catholic, Jewish, and Protestant programs do not face up to the challenge posed by modern education. What is called *education* is viewed as an appendage to the religious organization's will to survive, spread, and succeed. The religious members may feel as if they were living in two worlds: the one they learn about in their general education and the one which the religious organization tries to pass on.

This problem of the religious body's neglecting education was the reason for the religious education movement, which tried the alternate route of beginning with education and then including religion. In the previous chapter I described the unsatisfactory result of that approach; the religious meaning got swallowed. Modern education stands ready to examine anything and everything. The bright light of criticism can be cast upon religious life so that religion, too, can be rationally comprehended. Religious conservatives objected to what was called a liberal approach. To treat the religious life impartially, neutrally, and objectively was to miss the point of what being religious means.

I wish I could announce a third approach to religious education which has never been tried. Such an announcement would probably be disingenuous. The best I can offer is to try adding some correctives to the two approaches that have already been tried. Neither the word *religious* nor the word *education* is as fixed in meaning as the above description might suggest. The religions are frequently told that they should make changes. It should not be overlooked that our understanding of the word *education* might also be in need of examination and change. The education that swallowed the religious in the religious education movement was not education in general. It was the specific form of education dominant in the first half of the twentieth century in the United States of America.

In relating the **religious** and the **education** of religious education it may not make a great difference which comes first. It is more important to set up a dialogical relationship so that the movement is **religious** to **education** to **religious**, or **education** to **religious** to **education**. Obviously the dialogue can and should go beyond the three contributions, but here I am indicating the beginning of a process. The field of religious education has to be born from a movement over several decades. No definition that I or anyone else can set down at this time in history will fully establish this field.

To work out the relationship between *religious* and *education*, I will pick up the thread of the last section in chapter 1, on religious language. I will advert briefly to **religious,** move then to **education,** and come back in more detail to **religious**. This sequence will allow me to draw some conclusions about the relation of **religious** and **education**. Then the fourth chapter will be mainly **religious**, the fifth chapter predominantly **education**, and the other chapters further dialogue between **religious** and **education**.

In the final section of the first chapter, I pointed out some of the peculiarities of religious language and religious imagery. Religious life cannot be comprehended in what Philip Wheelwright calls "steno" language.[1] Is God above or within? Anyone who gives a direct and simple answer to that question has little understanding of how language operates in religious matters. Christian theology and Christian doctrine do tend to take on the characteristics of a literal, discursive, and factual language. That direction can be of some use, but the religious part of religious education cannot start there. Ten years ago I wrote that religious education has to be born from the meeting of education and theology.[2] I would like to correct that statement; religious education is born from the meeting of education and religion. Theology is only one form that religious language can take.

Religious language is peculiar and variegated because it does not reduce the world to facts and opinions. It refuses to accept reason (in its modern sense) and faith (meaning beliefs) as the way to comprehend the world. Jewish, Christian, and other religious traditions do not attempt to get at the real by gathering up all the facts and then applying a system of control. Religions have maintained that truth and order are available on a different basis. The way to deepest knowledge is neither rational nor irrational. The way to final order is neither will-ful nor will-less. One religious category for getting at this paradox is *revelation,* a peculiar notion described in chapter 4.

Modern education is liable to become impatient with this struggle with the limits of language. However, for education's own good it should respectfully consider that there might be some point to the millenia of experience in religious mysteries. If educational systems truly encountered the religious instead of trying to explain it away, a new modesty and reverence might surface in all education.

Two Models of Education

While keeping some peripheral awareness of the religious question, I now turn my main attention to education. Thousands of books have been written on education, so a few pages here may seem superfluous or presumptuous. Nevertheless, education, both in its nature and its aim, remains a murky issue. A consideration of education within a dialogue of the religious and the educational may throw a different light on this stubborn problem.

Education is, as R. S. Peters says, a "contestable" idea. Whatever anyone may say is the point of education, there is always someone ready to contest the idea. If John Dewey says that education is "growth," there will be numerous critics to respond that growth is too vague an image. Growth in what? Knowledge? Skills? Earning power? Any terms like these seem too narrow—which may be the reason why Dewey left things somewhat vague.

The meaning of the word *education* underwent a dramatic change about a century ago. I will presently go back to that earlier period. But during the past century education has had its meaning largely determined by its close association with the school. We may not be sure what education is, but we know you go to school to get some of it. As I pointed out in the first chapter, writers freely admit that education and school should be carefully distinguished, but the distinction never seems to work. When people try to expand the idea of education, we seem to sink into a sea of vague references to cultural and social organizations. At that point the experts in education bring us back to what we are confident is really education, namely, the school.

This circular route of discussion is not an accident. The ideal implicit in the modern usage of the word *education* finds expression in the school to the extent that whatever be the aim of education, it will be defined in school terms. The periodic rebellions against the dominance of school as the only form of education usually do not get free of the identification of education and school. Ivan Illich, for example, led one brief charge against a "schooled society" but succeeded not at all in breaking the connection or even in stating the question more clearly.

The trap is already sprung when we try to answer the question: What is the aim of education? As soon as we try to supply an answer, education has been reduced to an object, thing, or commodity. And immediately a school will appear that is willing to market the product. Periodically we get frustrated by an institution which treats education as a marketable commodity, but attacking the institution only leads to other kinds of schools. One way of resisting this process is to keep the aim stated in a global phrase ("the whole person," "the good life"), but eventually the aim gets translated into "objectives"—knowledge, skills, values, self-awareness, and so on.

Educational discussions almost invariably assume that school is the form. In fact, "formal education" is simply a complicated way to say "school." Since education necessarily denotes form, then definitions of education assume the school as reference point. Educational descriptions concern themselves with what the teacher does or what the student gets. Thus, education is defined as the _____ you do to get _____ result. In what is only a slight variation (but what is often proclaimed to be a revolutionary change) education is defined as the _____ result you get from doing _____ .

Much of the "contestableness" of educational writing concerns what to put in the blanks. The "_____ you do" draws the lesser amount of controversy, but is nonetheless important. The primary insert is likely to be "intentionality," that is, it is not education unless it is intentionally and deliberately planned. The teacher has to aim at a hoped-for result and use the appropriate means to get there. If the results can be scientifically tested, all the better. Of course, the intentionality of the teacher is related to the other blank. Here there is endless discussion of what is the aim or end of education. As I have noted, educational literature moves from high blown phrases ("the art of living," "ethical man," "quality of life") to mundane things that can be taught, tested, and credentialed (knowledge, skills, values).

I would like to contest this whole model of education rather than argue over what goes into the two blanks in the definition. The discussion of this model (the _____ you do to get _____ results) is simply not taking us far enough in understanding the educational problem which besets us today. But a real change of educational models would require facing up to the religious question. Modern education, almost by definition, has been a secular affair, that is, it has held out the hope that life could be made manageable in this world. The religious issue is an unwelcome reminder to educational theorists that education, in its modern meaning, is ultimately a false hope.

Before offering an alternate model of education that includes the religious, I would like to illustrate the problem described above with two well known authors, Lawrence Cremin and Charles Silberman. Cremin is more aware of the problem in his attempt to define education. Silberman's *Crisis in the Classroom* simply quotes Cremin's definition of education, but the book as a whole perfectly illustrates what is wrong with education as it is defined by the above model.

Lawrence Cremin is one of our most distinguished historians of education. He has taught many of us to see education as a richer story than the history of the school in the past century. It is ironic, therefore, that Cremin's own definition is caught within the limits of the model "education is the _____ you do to get _____ results." He struggles to transcend what he senses is too narrow a definition, but by piling up qualifiers the definition merely becomes unwieldy. I am not questioning a casual phrase of Cremin's but a painstaking formula which he has repeatedly written and which he required his students to memorize:

> Education is that
> deliberate, systematic, and sustained *effort*
> to transmit, evoke, or acquire
> knowledge, attitudes, values, skills, or sensibilities
> as well as any outcomes of that effort.[3]

I have stressed the key word in the definition: *effort.* If one is trying to be as comprehensive as possible about education, why would anyone start by saying "education is . . . effort"? The answer seems to be that education assumes a form in the modern world, and within that form one can only ask: What does the teacher do to produce educated students? A plausible answer to that question is indeed that the teacher must make an effort. Or as Cremin says in other places, what makes it education (as opposed to incidental learning) is intentionality and deliberateness. But Cremin knows better than most of us that the history of education is the history of people, environment, institutions, and traditions. It includes effort (and outcomes) but only as a minor part of the story. However, having locked himself into "effort," he can only struggle to free himself with three adjectives before the noun, three verbs after it, five nouns as objects and a phrase on outcomes. I am afraid that Cremin's own efforts here are being expended in the wrong direction. One can never get to a very rich meaning of education if one begins with "education is . . . effort."

My second illustration is Charles Silberman's *Crisis in the Classroom,* a much publicized and very disappointing study.[4] This large book makes its crucial choice in the first five pages, and after that the author never looks back. He adopts Cremin's definition of education while announcing that his interest is not merely school but all education. He then cites things in the culture besides school that educate. The list has more than a dozen items and includes Boy Scouts and social work. Having suggested to the reader that this route leads to endless proliferation and a chaos of data, Silberman pulls back to the one thing in the twentieth century we are sure is education: the school. Why are we sure that the school is education? Because that is where people deliberately and purposefully educate; school is where the effort is made.

Silberman, like Cremin, thinks that intentionality is the key factor in education. That may sound reasonable, but an intense concern with that one element hides much of what is going on. One should not forget Nietzsche's dictum that the most important part of human activity is what is not intended. In Silberman's case, intentionality roots him exclusively in the school, but the school itself remains opaque so long as one studies only intention and deliberate purpose. Silberman's main conclusion seems to be that some schools run well because they have principals who support their teachers. He also makes the charge that schools are "mindless" which, whatever the merits of the accusation, indicates what he was looking for. My complaint is not that he decided to study the school as part of education, but that he failed to see the school. Looking mainly at intention and effort, he has little to say about the relation of the school to the family, the neighborhood, the job site. Once education has been defined as effort and outcomes, the structural issues become invisible. The choice then is simply between the redundancy "formal education" and amorphousness; the only real question is how hard are teachers and administrators working to produce "outcomes" in the students.

I turn now to the second model of education—a model which has several well-defined forms. With the forms clearly named, it becomes unnecessary and undesirable to name the final product. In fact, one function of the interplay of forms is to prevent any thing, product, or commodity from becoming the aim of education.

As a first step in describing an alternate model it is helpful to note in the Oxford English Dictionary that up to the nineteenth century the word *education* had a wide meaning. It could even include plants and animals. What was valuable in a society was passed on to the next generation. As

Lawrence Cremin, Bernard Bailyn, and others have documented, the eighteenth-century colonies had definite forms of education besides schooling. For example, apprenticeship was a major part of education, and even young women who did not learn a trade served a kind of apprenticeship beyond the family. Whether we can retrieve a premodern meaning of any term is always questionable, but at the least one point should be clear, namely, those of us who try to name forms of education besides schooling are not engaged in a silly, contemporary fad. For most of its history the human race has used several well-defined forms of learning by which society tried to pass on what had been previously learned.

According to R. S. Peters, the meaning of education underwent a drastic change in the Industrial Era of the nineteenth century.[5] He pinpoints two striking developments: (1) the emergence of "the educated man" as the ideal of education, (2) the concentration upon knowledge as the indubitable value in education. Peters seems to think that the first point represents progress and that the newer meaning is simply more specific. The sexism of "the educated man" does not seem to bother him, but I think it is symptomatic of a bias in the specifying. Regarding the second point, Peters notes that it led to our split between "liberal education and vocational education"; here, too, Peters sees progress, but I think it is an unfortunate kind of progress.

Peters has made some interesting discoveries about an earlier meaning of *education* from which we might learn something today. We cannot return to an earlier era, and it does no good to pine nostalgically for a simpler past. The developments Peters cites are almost certainly irreversible. Nonetheless, we could carry these developments further by restoring their contexts: (1) We could situate the ideal of "the educated man" in the context of women, animals, and plants; let us continue to educate individuals but with full awareness of ecology. (2) We could examine the way liberal learning is used to maintain class bias; let us have both academic and manual learning for everyone.

I come then to a description of an alternate model of education. In this case *education is the* _____ *set of forms whose controlled interplay issues in* _____ . The blanks indicate that there is room for debate about what the forms are and what the outcome is. However, the debate will begin from two things already established: (1) The first blank refers to some finite set of interacting forms; that fact excludes both a single form and an endless procession of forms. Instead of the typical line "education is whenever people learn, but let us get to formal education," the question is: "What are those forms of learning which deserve our main attention and might be better shaped?" (2) The second blank indicates that education has a direction; however, what cannot be put in the blank is the name of some object or commodity. *Education does not have as its aim the attainment of any thing.*

Each of these two points deserves further comment. As to which are the forms of education, the question does not refer to institutions in addition to school but forms of learning which include schooling. Not everyone will agree on the naming but it is important to try giving names to three, four, or some number of forms that can realistically encompass the whole picture. An almost exact parallel is the use of the word *ministry* in the Catholic church today. In the English translation of the main index of Vatican II the word *ministry* does not appear, and under the word *minister* one reads: "see clergyman." Since Vatican II, of course, enormous energy has gone into broadening the meanings of *minister* and *ministry*. Catholic usage today converges with Protestant uses that extend the word *ministry* to almost anything ("the Christian's ministry in the world"), but one person is still called *the* minister. There is a "formal ministry" and also an endless number of ministries that do not break the identification of minister and clergyman. The only way that the distinction can come about is by naming the three, four, or five things which a church is supposed to do. Each ministry would have form, financial support, and a name. No one would be called *the* minister because there would be several kinds of ministers. I will return to the question of ministry and its relation to education in chapter 7.

In describing education one cannot consult the Gospels or the Acts of the Apostles as one might in defining church ministries. However, we can consult the history of past ages as well as current society to see how people learn and where they learn. One way to describe the overall pattern of learning is to note the sequence nearly everyone shares: family life, schooling, work, retiring. Those elements were in past Western society and are still with us. The Hindus speak of four stages of education which form a similar pattern.

The identification of these four areas is only a first step. We need to introduce distinctions that will give effective shape to education. For example, to be born into a family is to experience a specific kind of communal learning and physical training; to go to school is to learn about a bigger world through the medium of books; to have a job is to make a specific kind of vocational contribution which in turn shapes our lives; to retire is to discover a way of learning and of being through stepping into the quiet center of the universe. What seems to me the main problem is that these forms of learning are almost entirely age-segregated. There is probably a wisdom in the emphasis on schooling for children, but today schooling should also be available to adults. The retreat or retirement of older people has an obvious logic, but that element should be part of the life of younger people too. We need the communal experience in childhood, but we need something comparable later both from the family and other groups. In each case here there are values which are universal in scope but which find embodiment in partial and sometimes competing institutions. The forms of learning emerge in the tension of the following pairs. The form of education comes about through the interplay of all the elements:

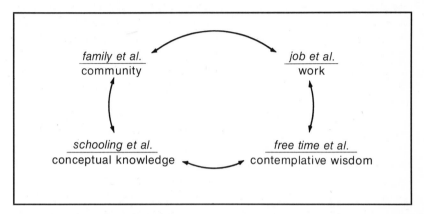

On the second point above and concerning the second blank in the description, I have said that education demands a direction but not a product. This is easier said than done because if deliberate intention is highlighted, then some object will inevitably become the aim of education. How can one intend if there is nothing to intend to? The answer is that the interplay of forms goes in a definite direction, but the direction is not wholly dependent on anyone's intention. Forms, which are in part the result of our ancestors, guide us and also remind us that we are not the creators of the world. Here is where the religious element comes into the picture to warn us against a fantasy of creating "the educated man." Modern revolutions that promise freedom are forced into describing some ideal state of affairs. Even Marxism which speaks constantly of the dialectic of history still looks forward to that final stage beyond class conflict.

What the religious can do in education is help us to accept our finitude (our forms). While we make efforts to transcend our limits, we know that we will always be creatures, not the creator. Religions that direct worship to the one God, by the same command forbid any strange gods—including an end to education. John Dewey was on the right track by casting the aim of education into the image of growth. Dewey's principle for what should be included in the curriculum was this: anything that will make us want to learn more. Dewey could never get more precise than that because, despite interest in the religious, he was in rebellion against the particular forms of religiousness he encountered, especially church dogma. As a result Dewey's aim of growth easily becomes a banal generality or else an overly intense activism.

Strange as it might sound to modern ears, education for its own good, even for its own definition, needs the religious. A richer religious life that includes contemplative prayer, liturgical ritual, and paradoxical speech could enliven the discussion of all education. Instead of saying that the aim of education is growth, a religious person might say that it is never to stop learning. Religious traditions know that the knowledge education should be concerned with is not just the knowledge we can acquire but the knowledge we must listen and wait for—perhaps at prayer, perhaps in a nursing home. Religions know that the freedom we can hope for is not liberation from the earth or the dominance of necessity but acceptance of our finite selves in a dying and rising universe.

I have used the word *interplay* to refer to the forms of learning. We play with what is given to us, although for a religious person play is serious activity. The interplay of people and environment has an abundance of intentionality, but it is often difficult to assign an origin to the intention. A mother may intend the educational effect in her child but very often she is acting in a way acquired from her mother who learned it from her mother. Who intends the effect of a fairy tale? The intention of the living person is a small part of the intentionality of generations of human beings. Surely most of what is learned in the family has little relation to what parents intend, but it is not incidental; it follows from the form of family life. I am not saying that parents are at fault. On the contrary, I think it is a fortunate and relaxing characteristic of human life that education does not primarily depend on my intention and effort. All I can do by my own efforts is give a gentle direction to the forces of education which the past bequeaths to us every day.

The Religious Challenge of Uniqueness

I have noted that religious language can have peculiar characteristics which set it at odds with the first model of education. However, in the second model of education, religious practices and religious language are not only allowed but welcome. If we wish to educate the whole human being, then the religious can remind us to keep open the receptive as well as the active, the interpersonal as well as the possessive, the cosmic as well as the social. If education does all that, then we become "more human" and "more ourselves" but in ways that no one can predict in detail. The first model promises to reduce conflict by enlightening each individual and reaching a state of social and political equality. The second model is likely to be less optimistic about eliminating social evils, but it is concerned with the ultimate question of the individual's relation to the universe.

In coming back to the religious side of the dialogue I would like to examine a single category which will show the conflict of religion with much of modern education. At the same time, this notion is helpful in further understanding what I have said about the interplay of forms and the direction of the second model of education. One of the most central and most confusing claims of religion is the claim to uniqueness. Like so many key terms, the word has two meanings that are almost opposites. People are in fact in a search for uniqueness; they are not interested solely in equality or enlightenment. As much or more than in the past, people want their lives to be something special. When separated from the paradoxes of religion, their search can be futile and even destructive of social cohesion. I offer as a challenge to education that it be able to comprehend in its definition the search for uniqueness.

Arnold Toynbee represents a common position on religion today: "We ought also, I should say, try to purge our Christianity of the traditional Christian belief that Christianity is unique . . . We have to do this if we are to purge Christianity of the exclusive-mindedness and intolerance that follows from a belief in Christianity's uniqueness."[6] Note that, far from attacking Christianity, Toynbee—like a reasonable, modern man—wishes only to "purge" Christianity of a minor quirk: its claim to uniqueness.

Most adherents of this religious group see this characteristic as indispensable. The issue is not a traditional and optional belief that can be conveniently discarded. The Lausanne Assembly of conservative Christians in 1974 reaffirmed the "uniqueness and universality of Christ." The sixth chapter of Karl Rahner's *Foundations of Christianity* uses the word several hundred times. In that book, as in most theology books, the word is relentlessly used but never examined. Before asking whether the claim can be defended we need to examine this peculiar word. Perhaps Toynbee is correct that *Christianity* is not the noun to follow unique. Nonetheless, the claim to uniqueness is indispensable to a Christian church.

Lewis Thomas has written: "We tend to think of ourselves as the only unique creatures in nature, but it is not so. Uniqueness is so commonplace a property of living things that there is really nothing at all unique about it."[7] In that playful second sentence Thomas has contrasted the two meanings of the term *unique*. These two are not contradictory because there is a common note that holds them together. From that point they go in opposite directions. When people use the word *unique* they sometimes have one meaning clearly in mind, but often the conflicting meanings have not been sorted out.

The two meanings of *unique* are united in the denotation "to differ from all the others." In one case what is unique differs from all the others by a process of exclusion. In the second case what is unique differs from all others by a process of inclusion. The two cases can be illustrated by these sequences:

1) **a, b, c, d**
2) **a, ab, abc, abcd**

In the first case, **d** is unique in the set of elements **a, b, c, d.** It shares no common characteristics with **a, b, c.** In the second case, **abcd** is unique in the set **a, ab, abc, abcd.** It is the only element which includes the elements **a, b, c.** It is uniquely different by being like all the other elements.

Important to note is that in both cases we are dealing with limit situations. That is, the cases approach indefinitely close to a point but never reach it. When we say that something is unique we point in one of two directions.

In case one, **d** is unique with respect to whatever **a, b, c** stand for. But to the extent, for example, that **a, b, c, d** are all letters then **d** is not "entirely unique." If we change the sequence to **a, b, c, 9,** then the fourth element no longer shares the characteristic of being a letter, but it is still a written sign. There is no such thing as a unique thing because the thing will at least share the characteristic of thingness with other things. Things can approach uniqueness by the process of exclusion but they do not ever get there. The comparative "more unique" is not quite accurate. Unique is a limit that is never reached, but things can be "more nearly unique." We commonly call some things *unique* because we have assumed a set of reference which may indeed have only one element.

The second example is more obviously a limit case: **a, ab, abc, abcd** immediately suggests that there could be **a, ab, abc, abcd, abcde.** That would mean **abcd** is not entirely unique. If novelty and history are allowed, then there is nothing which is truly unique by inclusion. The last possibility in history could conceivably be unique, but "it" would have a receptive character that we are unfamiliar with in our experience. However, we do experience the direction of this uniqueness first in living things and distinctly in persons. Common speech rightly uses the word *unique* as descriptive of human individuality.

This second meaning is not less precise than the first. Things maintain their reality by excluding other things. Persons (and other living things to a lesser degree) individualize by going in the opposite direction. The human being is an astounding paradox which the word *unique* describes. The drive inherent to the human is to become everything while not ceasing to be oneself. No human being achieves that aim while on earth, but the process is so distinctly human that the word *unique* applies to every person.

Common speech also recognizes that some people are "more unique" than others. The more a person embodies his or her people or the historical era, the more readily the word *unique* comes to mind. When it was said of Cromwell that he was the most typical Englishman of his time because he was the oddest, the peculiar logic of uniqueness is evident. Erik Erikson's description of Luther shows the same logic: "An individual may be called upon (called by whom only the theologians claim to know, and by what only bad psychologists) to lift his individual patient-hood to the level of a universal one and to try to solve for all what he could not solve for himself alone."[8] Luther became distinctly individual by his receptiveness to all; his case is universal because it is unique.

The story of Luther is unthinkable before the story of Jesus of Nazareth. Our meaning of person (and the full meaning of uniqueness) emerged with Jesus and reflection upon him. The reason why *unique* is so appropriately used of Jesus is that it was through that person's existence that the meaning of uniqueness was invented or discovered. This fact does not mean that Jesus was "entirely unique"; no person could be. But in making human beings aware that this meaning does exist, the uniqueness of Jesus can be a key to the inclusive uniqueness of universal history.

Instead of their being in opposition, uniqueness and universality arose together. Anyone who wishes to reach out to universal history by eliminating uniqueness should reconsider their common origins. A liberal theologian writes: "An insistence on the uniqueness of the historical Jesus can only be a hindrance. . . . It is just too preposterous to believe that God gave her/his world embracing love uniquely through Jesus."[9] I don't believe he knows what he is saying. The uniqueness of the historical Jesus is practically a definition of terms. The author's argument ought to be with the claim to a "unique Christian revelation" or "unique Christianity," that is, the claim to uniquely exclusive things. Instead of denying uniqueness to Jesus, we should be busy affirming uniqueness in the lives of other great religious figures.

Uniqueness with reference to person has both Greek and Jewish roots. Religiously, it is a development within the idea of *chosen people* and should never be separated from that context. Jews have often been advised to give up the idea of *chosen* in our enlightened age of statistical averages. Yet despite the obvious risk of misunderstanding, the Jews have stubbornly held on to the term *chosen people*. At first glance the phrase seems to be a pretentious claim to superiority, but anyone slightly familiar with Jewish history knows it to be a paradoxical and ironic description of the Jews' sufferings and the Jewish relation to universal history.

Chosen people like *unique person* is something of a redundancy. To be chosen is to be a people; to be unique is to be a person. Peoplehood arose from a sense of chosenness. Judaism at its best and richest knows that the real chosen people are all people. Jews are the "chosen people's people"; they stand in for humanity for the sake of humanity. Uniqueness is a further development *within* this religious notion. The Christian church at its best has been the affirming of every unique person in the chosen people.

Jesus' own Jewish community and the Jewish people of today have to be affirmed by Christian language. If one eliminates the Jewishness from Jesus, then the assertion of uniqueness does become arrogant and exclusivistic because, despite protests to the contrary, one is now talking about things not persons. For their part, Jews might find most of what is said of Jesus by the church to be a legitimate strand within Judaism. Christians and Jews also need to recognize that *chosen people* is a concept to be explored outside Jewish and Christian history. Islam and North American Native religions have their own developments of *chosen people.*

The Christian church affirms God and the uniqueness of human history through Jesus, the Christ. The doctrine says nothing against how other people may come to God and universal history. It is not necessary for the Christian church immediately to claim that Jesus is the "most nearly unique." This is a question that can be submitted to dialogue and comparison. If church people encounter God's presence in Jesus and Christian tradition, let them affirm that as strongly as they can and try to share that with others. Precisely because it should be reaching out to the whole world, the church has to hold on to the uniqueness of Jesus and thereby the uniqueness of every human being.

Conclusion

From the preceding discussion of religious and education a few principles can be established for a field of religious education:

1) The religious in religious education has to be concrete, particular, "nearly unique." The religious cannot consist of a lowest common denominator or abstract generalities. The false hope of so much modern education has been to retain a nice-sounding religious sentiment but to get rid of the divisive doctrines. Anyone with more than a casual interest in religion immediately sees through the ploy. Most religious groups in their internal language lay claim to the only God there is, to the one true faith,

and to the only way to salvation. Religious education cannot dismiss these claims as outmoded superstitions and still think it is dealing with the religious life.

A sensitive educator should be able to get inside a tradition and understand its peculiar form of language. That is perhaps easier to do with the religious tradition one has been reared in, although some degree of "passing over" to other religious traditions is clearly possible. Sometimes we understand our own religious syntax better after having studied someone else's. In any case, we cannot master a language without grasping its inner connections and getting a feel for the idioms. The religious way of speaking is a grasping for the unique/universal; the attempt never fully succeeds and will usually sound intolerant to anyone beyond the group.

In the eighteenth century Edmund Burke could still defend the positive meaning of the word *prejudice*, but his position was in the process of losing out.[10] As Hans Gadamer has put it, "the fundamental prejudice of the Enlightenment was the prejudice against prejudice."[11] Religious claims are prejudicial in the ancient sense that they are judgments not arrived at by one's own rational search. Whether any religious claim leads to prejudice in the contemporary and negative sense should not be judged too quickly. I have pointed out that the Jews as "chosen people" and Jesus as "the unique revelation of God" make sense in context and need not be abandoned. The group has to be careful in distinguishing between statements internal to the group (e.g., in liturgical readings) and statements directed beyond the group. Some doctrines could be explained today, but it would probably not be worth the effort. For example, the doctrine "outside the church there is no salvation" could merely be a definition of *church,* but such twisting of a word against its obvious meaning would not be helpful. A more basic reconstruction of this and many other doctrines is necessary. We need an educational setting to work intelligently, patiently, and reverently at the reconstruction of religious doctrines.

2) The aim in establishing a field of religious education is not some grand synthesis. No union of the major traditions is on the horizon. The aim of religious education is greater appreciation of one's own religious life and less misunderstanding of other people's. When people of different religious backgrounds meet in an educational setting the almost inevitable result is stronger confirmation in one's own religious tradition.

I said above that Christians do not know what they mean by the uniqueness of Jesus unless they understand the Jewish claim to be chosen people. The converse can also be true. John Murray Cuddihy quotes Balfour Brickner: "It is ironic that truly theological dialogue with Christians might be a catalyst which helps Jews stay alive Jewishly." Jewish rediscovery of chosen people out of dialogue with Christians is ridiculed by Cuddihy because he assumes that the claims of Jews and Christians are incompatible. But what is incompatible or compatible between Catholic and Protestant, Christian and Jewish, Jewish and Muslim, Eastern and Western, no one yet knows. Only a setting of religious education could slowly reveal both what is actual and what is possible in religious agreements.

3) Within the total process of religious education there should be a place for passing on the past. Most of that work has to be done nonverbally through ritual, but part of it can be done through the study of history. In educational writing of recent decades there has been a strong bias against *traditioning,* that is, the handing over of the wisdom of the last generation to the next. Religious people should be among those who know that this attitude is irrational (though it is expressed in very rational terms) and a distortion of most of the history of education. If it is to remain human, education has to avoid the impression that the world was invented in the twentieth century.

This position deserves to be called conservative, but religiously the word has been captured by those who engage in "nonhistorical orthodoxy." Instead of conserving and passing on a way of life, they get obsessed with catechisms, doctrinal formulas, and biblical texts. Scripture and doctrine are helpful to tradition but only as secondary reflection upon religious attitudes and practices. The teaching of religion in the school setting is an indispensable part of religious education in the contemporary world, but it is not enough to sustain a religious life. Each of the several forms of learning described in my second model of education has a part to play in preserving, continuing, and enriching the religious life. Educational theorists who concentrate on intentionality and deliberateness might profitably examine in the light of religious history whether they might be missing the larger picture of education.

4
Teaching
Within Revelation

The field of religious education requires a dialogue between the religious and the educational. In a genuine dialogue both parties change to some degree without abandoning their respective pasts. The deeper past may have something to say to the more immediate past. One of the sources for my alternate model of education is education's forgotten past. As I indicated in the previous chapter, the religious cannot survive a system in which education is assumed to be a commodity available through schools. However, when education is conceived as an interplay of learning forms then the religious quest is integral to education, and education is the richer for this change.

On the religious side of the dialogue the change required is no less a challenge. The first effect of education on religion may seem destructive because critical questions are asked and doubts are raised. For example, what is education to make of the Catholic church's doctrine of infallibility? If the response is that one must accept it because it is from God, that is not a sufficient answer for education. The educator would wish to dig further into the meaning of the claim that any doctrine is accepted because it is from God. The Catholic church's doctrine of infallibility might be seen as one expression of the religious group's understanding of itself and its mission. A parallel claim in Islam is the saying "my community cannot be in error." The point of education is not to subvert such doctrines but to understand them. The official guardians of authority in any religious group are understandably wary of teachers who dig at the roots of cherished notions and traditional rites. Nevertheless, a religious group today needs the challenge and the context of education.

If we pursued the example in the above paragraph it would lead us to the fundamental claim in Judaism, Christianity, Islam, and other religions, namely, that what we say is true not because of our authority but because God says so. If this claim can be secured, then the followers of Islam, Christianity, or Judaism can with relative ease accept hundreds of doctrinal and moral prescriptions that the group maintains. This fundamental claim has been traditionally formulated in the idea of *divine revelation*. One might expect that there would be numerous treatises today on the intelligibility of the notion of revelation and on the historical development of the claim to being a recipient of divine revelation. What we find is something different.

A peculiar thing has been happening to the word *revelation* in Christian theology: it has been disappearing. Anyone who wishes to verify this claim needs only to look at the index or text of most theology books in recent years. As a general rule, the more liberal the theology is, the less the word *revelation* is used.

Conservative writers like Carl Henry have no hesitation in commenting on the word *revelation*.[1] Further to the right, Sun Myung Moon and others use the word more aggressively than ever. In contrast, the word *revelation* is nearly absent in liberal theology. I should think that this fact would invite comment on all sides. Surely the near disappearance of such a central category must have some significance for the Christian churches and religious study.

I indicated above that the word *revelation* had *almost* disappeared in liberal Christian theology. That fact is perhaps more troublesome than if the word were entirely absent. Absence might indicate that the word is no longer necessary or that it had been replaced by a more useful word. Instead, Christian theology still assumes that there is a Christian revelation but one looks in vain for an exposition of the meaning and coherence of the concept.[2]

The literature of religious education in the churches does not show the same embarrassment with the word *revelation*. In fact, the word has probably become more prominent in recent years, especially in Roman Catholic writing. How does one explain this contrast? Is religious education literature simply a step behind theological writing? Or is religious education groping toward a new meaning which is beyond the view of Christian theology?

I am not certain that the second response is an accurate one. But in the hope that religious education may be already discovering a wider and deeper meaning for the word *revelation,* this essay will try to contribute to the exploration. My central proposal is that revelation is better approached as an *aesthetic* than a *scientific* category. What I will oppose is the use of the word *revelation* as a scientific or pseudoscientific category. It is this scientific meaning of revelation in Christian theology that has become indefensible, a fact that is implicity admitted by theology's embarrassed silence.

The term *aesthetic* may not be fully adequate to my intention. However, it does convey some alternative way of feeling, knowing, and behaving. Three characteristics of the aesthetic can be offered as a preliminary basis for the word's meaning: (1) Aesthetic activity pertains to concrete materials and does not abstract to a level of general ideas. The universal can be approached only through its embodiment in particular events, people, and things. (2) Aesthetic knowing is neither rational nor irrational; it is reason and more than reason. (3) The aesthetic dimension is a concern for wholeness; truth is primarily sought not in statements about the world but in the person's interacting with the environment.

If the word *revelation* is useful as an aesthetic category it would indicate the *how* of religious education as much or more than the *what* of religious education. The word *revelation* would then encompass a style of teaching, a way of using books, film, music, and so on, a communal form of institution, and many other facets of education that are often neglected. In this context, religious education is not the teaching of a "content" first processed by Christian theology. The content of religious education would no longer be under the control of theology; as *educational* content the material can come from a great variety of sources that help to clarify a religious life. For example, science fiction novels are a rich source of religious writing in our day, as is also true of a number of recent plays on death.

In advocating an aesthetic meaning of revelation I am acutely aware of the sloppiness and irrationality that can easily substitute for the scientific. I sympathize with these sentiments of James Hillman:

> The movement from one side of the brain to the other, from tedious daily life in the supermarket to supraconsciousness, from trash to transcendence, the "altered state of consciousness" approach—to put it all in a nutshell—denies the historical ego. It is an approach going back to Saul, who became Paul, conversion into the opposite, knocked off one's ass in a flash.[3]

Whether Hillman is fair to St. Paul may be debatable, but certainly the problem he is describing has never been more apparent than it is today. The splits of rationalism/irrationalism or historical ego/mystical absorption are accompanied by "conversions" which do nothing to heal the splits.

There are two main defenses against being caught in these inhuman splits and false conversions: (1) Learn something about the history of the terms one is using. (2) Develop an educational setting adequate to the exploration of these human mysteries. If religious education is to make fruitful use of the word *revelation* then it has to know some of the historical meanings of the word. The retrieval of meaning can begin within one's own Christian history, though if pursued far enough it will lead to meaning beyond that history. I shall first sketch some of that history and then offer some conclusions for religious study and some educational implications.

Historical Considerations

In the earliest period of Christian history the word *revelation* was used to cap the entire process by which the problem of the human condition was resolved. Humans had been looking for a way out, a resolution to human affairs. The people who were called Christians announced that they had the answer. God had taken a personal interest and intervened on behalf of the race. Within the Christian scheme Israel had been the preparation, and Jesus the risen Lord was the culmination. In one of the patristic images, Jesus "recapitulated" the process, becoming a summary of past history and a foreshadowing of the future.

Isolated texts of St. Paul may make him sound like a twentieth-century kook, but the whole Pauline corpus fits into a thought-out pattern for the human race. Such an ambitious viewpoint was not without its riddles and paradoxes. The "Christian view" led immediately into disagreement, debate, and church disarray. The last book of the Bible, *Revelation,* was for centuries considered unintelligible, but it reemerged as a key to prophetic interpretation in the Protestant Reformation.

When the word *revelation* was used in the early church, it did not refer to something contained in the Bible or the biblical text itself. Rather, *revelation* was one of several words (e.g., *dispensation, economy, salvation*) that could refer to the entire divine plan of things. The word *revelation* emphasized the element of *knowing*. The Christians claimed to know the way to God (or God's way to us) because they possessed a key to interpreting the universe.

The line-up of the competitors appeared to be: *philosophy and (pagan) religion vs. (the) (Christian) revelation.* There wasn't a *Christian* revelation as opposed to other revelations. There was simply a revelation of God which took precedence over all human attempts of philosophy and religion. Almost immediately, as the Christian claims encountered education and classical learning, some realignment began to occur. The reinterpretation of Christian claims has continued to this day. But whereas the church has made political, social, and other kinds of adjustments, the claim to possess the revelation of God has never been adequately addressed.

The Middle Ages saw the emergence of reason, not as an equal partner with revelation, but as a negotiator. Reason, particularly as represented by pagan philosophy, was not an enemy of revelation. Human rationality was a reflection of that divine reason which illuminates the universe. The human ability to reason, it was thought, is limited by reason's being located in a bodily creature. Furthermore, human reason is distorted by the existence of sin. Revelation adds to and corrects the knowledge of human beings.

In the work of Thomas Aquinas the interplay of reason and revelation is complex and careful. Aquinas wished to give every credit possible to reason, incorporating into his "Christian philosophy" the body of classical learning as he knew it. Reason could not be undercut or substituted for, but it did find fulfillment in (the) (Christian) revelation. Neither reason nor revelation referred primarily to processes inside the human head. Reason and revelation were ways of being in the world and of human participation in a divine pattern.

The period after the Renaissance, Reformation, and Scientific Revolution represents a decisive change in the Christian use of the word *revelation*. The main field of interest became interiorized, and the discussion was about reason and faith. The word *revelation* was still used, functioning now as the object of faith. That object was now in some dispute. For centuries the Protestant-Catholic conflict was formulated as "Scripture alone" vs. "Scripture and tradition" as the place of revelation. That difference was a minor one compared to the fundamental agreement between Protestant and Catholic, viz., that revelation is an object located somewhere.

To cope with the era in which the churches found themselves, Christian theology conceived of itself as a science in the modern sense of the word. Theology could use the same stringent controls of reasoning as the other sciences, but it could outdo them in one respect: its premises were absolutely certain because they came directly from God. As befits a science, theology proper did not have to examine revelation because revelation was a premise, and premises are assumed in science. The pretheological defense of the concept of revelation was largely an examination of the credibility of the Bible (and, for Catholics, tradition) as a source of truths.

Looking back on the period of modern Christian theology, one can see a missed step in the assumptions about revelation. The theologian assumed that the method of modern science was the game to be played. That assumption entailed the existence of data (the given object) to be reasoned from. "The Christian revelation" now functioned as "the given" for the science of theology. Arguments about *where* that revelation was located and *who* was final interpreter obscured the more important development, viz., the assumption that there was a thing called "the Christian revelation."

If the premise could be assumed, then the science of Christianity was impregnably strong. A divine science provided total security and absolute certitude. Charles Finney, one of the most influential preachers in the nineteenth-century United States, could say: "I had read nothing on the subject except my Bible and what I had there found. . . . I had interpreted as I would have understood the same or like passages in a law book."[4] By the 1950s the scientific model had shifted from law to psychology but the guarantee of certainty was the same. In one of the best-selling books of that decade, Norman Vincent Peale presented Christianity as having "the characteristics of a science in that it is based upon a book which contains a system of techniques and formulas designed for the understanding and treatment of human nature."[5]

The continuance of this science for "the understanding and treatment of human nature" rested upon the accommodation which Christian churches had made in the seventeenth and eighteenth centuries. Since there were two sources of knowledge, faith and reason, there were bound to be conflicts. Neither church spokesmen nor scientists in the early modern period wished to incite open warfare. In the English-speaking world John Locke provided the acceptable solution in his influential essay, *The Reasonableness of Christianity.* One should note not only the first but the last word of the title. "Christianity," a word connoting a self-enclosed system of ideas, was largely an invention of the eighteenth century, and of course "Christianity" was, if anything, "reasonable."

John Locke may seem far away, but it is his accommodation that we are still using. Some of Locke's statements on the need for reason may sound similar to those of Thomas Aquinas, but the intervening five centuries had transformed the word *reason.* In Locke's world the two poles were not reason/revelation but reason/faith. Revelation entered the picture only as the "proposition" to which faith assented. From that starting point, revelation could only go in one direction, namely, in subordination to reason. "Faith," writes Locke, "is the assent to any proposition not . . . made by the deductions of reason, but upon the credit of the proposer, as coming from God, in some extraordinary way of communication. This way of discovering truths to men, we call *revelation.*"[6] Locke allows that revelation may be followed when it speaks of matters on which reason has nothing to say or when it deals with matters on which reason yields only probabilities. When reason conflicts with a supposed truth of revelation, it is reason that must be followed.

The Lockean solution seemed a "reasonable" one—which indeed it was. The catch was the shifting meaning of the word *reason* and the uses to which reason might be put. Anyone who did not go along with the accommodation of "Christianity" and modern science was pushed to the fringe of social acceptability. The legacy of the eighteenth century to the centuries that have followed is the choice between a cool, liberal, reasonable religion and a hot, reactionary, irrational religious life.

Reasonable gentlemen like Ben Franklin could never understand all the fuss about religion. If people wanted some religion, let them have it so long as we all remain civil and rational. People who knew that there was something wrong with this choice but who could not restate the issue became increasingly shrill. By the beginning of the twentieth century, Billy Sunday was screaming across the land: "Thousands of college graduates are going as fast as they can straight to hell. If I had a million dollars I'd give $999,999 to the church and $1 to education. . . . When the word of God says one thing and scholarship says another, scholarship can go to hell."[7]

We look back condescendingly to Billy Sunday and his era, but it is not clear that our era has progressed to another plane of understanding. For much of the twentieth century it seemed that Locke's reasonable solution was carrying the day. Reasonable religion was protected because it was useful and innocuous. Unreasonable religion was allowed because it was soon to disappear. There were signs as far back as World War I that this edifice was built on shifting sands. But it is in the last few decades that massive breaks have appeared in the structure. Faith/reason on the subjective side and science/reasonable Christianity on the objective are now threatened by chaotic upheavals.

Theoretical Conclusions

It would be nice if as conclusion to the above problem I could state the *right* answer. But I think that neither I nor anyone else at this juncture of human, religious, and Christian history can supply the answer. When a problem is so deeply immersed in historical complexity, then any words one might choose for an answer are already part of the problem. What one can do is propose radical surgery on one or two key terms that might offer a new route for exploration.

Christian theology cannot handle the issue by putting Band-aids on the word *revelation,* and neither can theology avoid the question. The premise of Christian theology is in question and for this problem theology is not the judge. The body of Christian theology needs to be placed in an educational setting where the arbiter is neither the "norms" of theology nor the "reason" of eighteenth-century Enlightenment. The educational judge is human experience conceived of as broadly and as deeply as human beings are capable.

1) My first conclusion is negative in form but ultimately positive in effect: the Christian churches do not possess an object that can be called "the Christian revelation." Centuries of defending the proposition that there does exist such an object have trickled down to embarrassment on the left and irrationality on the right. Liberal Christian theologians ought to feel some relief at this admission though they also need to recognize that the effect is revolutionary in religious studies. The word *revelation* cannot be

left to die quietly; its history needs to be studied. Possibly the word *revelation* has a future which is radically different from the one which modern theology assumed since the age of John Locke.

Some people get very angry at the suggestion to eliminate "the Christian revelation." I hope it is clear at this point that my argument is with the *words* "Christian revelation." There is no disparagement here of Christian Scripture/doctrine, the person of Jesus, or the symbols of church tradition. My argument is with identifying any or all of these things with the word *revelation.* Ontologically and epistemologically the term "Christian revelation" is a box from which no escape has been found.

From a more positive perspective, letting go of "the Christian revelation" allows a reappropriation of early Christian history as well as a dialogue with other religions. The unwise attempt to complement Christian revelation with Buddhist revelation, Muslim revelation, and so on, only compounds the problem. The early church was right in looking for the one and only revelation. What we can see today is that the history of Hindu, Muslim, and other groups may with the Christian church be expressions or partial embodiments of that revelation.

The earliest Christian impulse was not to *have* the Christian revelation but to *be* the final revealing of God in the world. When it became evident that the world was not at its end, the church had to reconceive its position. The church could still think of itself as final or decisive or culminating. But the split with Judaism and the failure of educational/institutional reform to keep pace with its missionary zeal severely limited the church. It was forced into a position of defending "the Christian revelation," which in time came to mean the truths given to the church and not available elsewhere.

The long history of "Christian revelation" is understandable, but to perpetuate the inadequate language of another era is no longer defensible. One of Kierkegaard's images of faith (more attractive than some of his others) is of a man taking his foot from the bottom of the lake to see whether he will float on the water. There is no way to explore the usefulness of the word *revelation* if Christian theology still presumes that the word refers to an object under the control and definition of the church. Letting go of that solid ground might lead to swimming in a new ocean of philosophical and religious possibilities.

The elimination of the term "Christian revelation" does not lessen the importance of studying Jewish and Christian history. Jewish and Christian peoples have made special contributions to world history. Perhaps every people has made special contributions; that's mostly for them to say. The word *special* here doesn't necessarily entail a meaning of exclusivity. Jewish and Christian peoples have at their disposal more than a century of magnificent historical studies. Ironically, it was this very study of history (especially biblical history) together with further advances in science that helped to undermine the faith/reason accommodation of the eighteenth century.

2) With the upheaval of modern reason and its associates Christian faith/revelation, a new framework is urgently needed. In this setting, the word *revelation* may prove valuable if its ancient Greek, early Christian, medieval Catholic, and contemporary nonreligious meanings can be tapped. That is a tall order, of course, and the odds are probably against such a retrieval of meaning. Still, almost everything is now in question, and it may be the unlikely contender that will prove adequate to the job of encompassing the unity/diversity of today.

Revelation in this context is not a noun/object but an umbrella word for the total relational pattern. It is what I have called an aesthetic category. It would be a word not under the control of the Christian church but one in which the Christian church could participate. It is not immediately a religious word though it can obviously incorporate religious meaning. The word *revelation* does not imply any splits (cognitive/affective, active/passive, human/nonhuman), but it does connote elements of surprise and spontaneity. In short, it is not reducible to reason but neither is it irrational.

The word *revelation* is alive in contemporary writing outside church circles. It appears regularly in the daily newspaper, especially on the editorial page and in the movie review. It is also the word people use when they try to describe a momentous experience that goes beyond words. "It was an emotional shock; I recall an evening of profound revelation." (Piaget, on first reading Bergson.) "I suspect that every life moves full circle—toward revelation; you begin to see, and even rejoice to see what you always saw." (James Baldwin, on returning to the United States.) Unfortunately, *revelation* is also the word that feeds irrational tendencies in our world and it is laid claim to by anyone with messianic tendencies. "I have come to reveal something new. I want to share with you a new revelation from God." (Sun Myung Moon, in his first U.S. rally.)

The category of revelation, therefore, is not disappearing despite the impression one might get from Christian theology. On the topic of revelation, Christian life has more to offer than is apparent in the old style theology manual or even the Vatican II document on revelation. The Christian church could provide some of the philosophical and historical moorings which the idea of revelation needs. To get at the deeper roots of the issue, church writers have to let go of something. It has long been fashionable to attack a "propositional" notion of revelation only to replace it with a vaguer object that could still be called "the Christian revelation." My criticism has gone in an opposite direction, affirming the need for propositions but distinguishing propositions and every other object from revelation. Instead of being an object, revelation is a relation in which the human being participates. The full range of bodily and social response is intrinsic to the meaning of revelation. Although this *aesthetic* meaning of revelation would sound foreign to many church officials, I would like to think it would be intelligible to John the Evangelist, Thomas Aquinas, Meister Eckhart, Martin Luther, and great religious figures outside Christian history.

Educational Implications

1) Religious education may be defined as the attempt to keep education open to the undreamt possibilities of the human race. There is nothing vague or general about this description of religious education; the job is specific, urgent, and practical. The puzzle within this definition is *how* to do it. If possibilities have not even been dreamt, how can one keep open to them? The beginning of an answer to that question is found in this statement by G. K. Chesterton: "There is a thought that stops thought and that's the only thought that ought to be stopped." Instead of saying "be open," Chesterton calls attention to the particular closures of the mind which must be opposed. My only argument with Chesterton's statement is that thought is not directly available but language is. That is, there are words which close off reality, and those words need systematic resistance.

Thus speech that is sexist or antiecological obstructs the exploration of reality and the receptivity of the human being. For example, modern Christian theology consistently spoke of "man and God" or "man and nature." The language of contemporary religious education has to be "men, women, children, and others." The meaning of the religious and divine can only be found by examining the total interplay of man/woman, adult/child, human/nonhuman. The gradual purification of sexism, racism, ageism, and so on, is not a peripheral issue for religious education; it is what makes religious education possible at all. A *scientific* meaning of revelation presumed there was a body of knowledge that God had given to man. An *aesthetic* meaning of revelation is an invitation to discover the divine in the present experience of humans and nonhumans.

2) Religious education is a combination of silence and paradoxical speech. Speech originates and ends in silence; the crucial question is whether the final silence is empty or full. If one uses only modern reason and discursive speech, then the system completes itself at some boundary, and there is nothing more to be said. However, if words function as choreography for the human body in relation to artistic materials, then

silence emerges in the middle of life. Silence is also an inner moment of all education.

The basis of religious education is bodily and social ritual. In the face of both life and death, nonverbal gestures provide the essential stability for the human person. An education that is religious preserves important rituals that are salvageable from the past. Although the modern West is obsessed with the future, religious education ought to be a reminder that when it comes to the basic human gestures of living and dying, there are no wholly new answers. Religious education needs to deal with modern rationality neither by denying it nor by submitting to it. Religious education 'has to challenge modern reason to find its bodily and social roots in symbols, community, and bodily environment.

Within a context of community and ritual, the religious use of speech is a subverting of speech. That is, speech bends back upon itself leaving us speechless in the middle of a community. The parables and sayings of Jesus are not, as the eighteenth and nineteenth centuries supposed, a rational system of moral truths. Instead, they are extraordinary paradoxes of speech which do not fit the reason of modern times. In this respect, Christian doctrines are also enigmatic formulas whose chief function is to resist the reduction of Jewish and Christian stories to a finished system.[8]

3) The Christian expression of revelation is the life of church groups. In a *scientific* meaning, the church has a revelation; in an *aesthetic* meaning the revelation has a church. The form which the church has is not derivable from "the Christian revelation." But it is that very form of institutional life which is most powerfully educative (or miseducative). To return to the question of "undreamt possibilities," the form which church could take may not yet have been imagined.

When ecclesiastical form is deduced from an object which the church itself established, then little change is possible. The form necessarily tends to be individualistic, rationalistic, and bureaucratic. But if education were attentive to the very old and the very young, if education preserved and encouraged community, if education explored the entire range of symbolic and sacramental gestures, then a new institutional form might emerge. The purpose here is not to do violence to the Christian past but, on the contrary, to recover more of that past. The learning of exegetes and historians provides only the beginning of that education in what our past means within our present.

The task before religious education is breathtakingly large, but it is also urgent and unavoidable. Neither reason nor faith nor both can stem the tide of what is now enveloping the human. Modern Enlightenment has turned out to be a brief, illusory period in which a few humans (men) thought they were getting the world under control. The word *revelation* might have served as a healthy reminder of other forces, but the word became encapsulated in the idea system of the time. The concept of revelation is now exploding out of all apparent control. The appropriate educational response today is an artistic approach that incorporates rational structures within itself. To teach within revelation is to acknowledge that the world goes beyond one's control. But it is also to grasp that there are artistic structurings of experience which bring the human being into dialogue with other humans and with other beings who share the earth.

5
Teaching
Religion

In the previous chapters I have continually returned to the distinction between *education* and *school*. When this distinction is not clearly and consistently maintained, the religious life cannot get a fair hearing in education. If the school is the only place we turn to for the formation and development of a Christian (Jewish, Buddhist, Muslim) way of living, then the burden upon the school is intolerable, and the religious life suffers a reduction. In the next chapter I will examine the areas of work and leisure that need to complement the school. In this chapter I wish to give the school its due. While insisting that school is not the whole of education, I have also emphasized that schooling is a legitimate and indispensable form of learning. The teaching of religion in the context of the school is one crucial part of the field of religious education.

I wish to explore in this chapter what it means to teach religion. The obvious procedure would seem to be to examine those institutions that engage in the teaching of religion. That logical step runs into an immediate snag: there is no obvious place to turn to for examining the teaching of religion. This deficiency is indicative of the fact that a field of religious education is not yet fully developed.

The problem in this area can be illustrated by consulting the literature on religion and the public school. Several decisions of the U.S. Supreme Court in the early 1960s gave new impetus to discussing the place of religion in the public school. Some states immediately set about to design material for a religion curriculum. Overall, however, the progress has been painfully slow. The movement attracts only a small number of people, and it is not considered to be part of a field of religious education.

At the heart of this issue is the question: Is it possible to teach religion in the public school? The literature declares: No, one may only "teach about religion." This distinction is attributed to the Supreme Court, but the Court was itself drawing upon the religious education literature of the 1940s. The choice to "teach about religion" rather than to "teach religion" was an unhappy choice in 1940 and is an obstruction to thinking in the 1980s.

One of the writers responsible for the phrase was F. Ernest Johnson. He noted in 1940 that "studying *about* is the beginning of study. It is the way an orientation is effected. But such inquiry has in it the element of participation based on interest."[1] The teaching and studying would move from externals to deeper issues of religion in the lives of the students. I think Johnson was moving in the right direction, but, as he later recognized, his contrast did not capture his intention. By that time, however, the phrase "teach about religion" had become part of a 1947 committee report of the American Council on Education.[2]

The unfortunate thing about the phrase "teach about religion" is its implication that "teach religion" has already been clarified and found objectionable. As I have noted, it is difficult to find institutions that clearly and explicitly teach religion. An obvious place to explore the meaning of "teach religion" is the public school. But it will never be tried if the chief advocates of religion in the public school dismiss teaching religion as objectionable and illegal before they begin.

Religion has always been intertwined with the schools of the United States of America. In the public system that came to triumph in the 1840s there was a concentrated effort to avoid the divisiveness of religion. Thus elements that were thought to be part of a common religion in the country held a prominent place in the schools. Reading from the Bible became a regular practice in many parts of the country. Rituals and prayers were commonly practiced in the schools. What the school did not do with religion was *teach* it. Ironically, educators who are designing religion curricula today still deny that the public school can teach religion.

A main reason why people interested in the public school want no part of teaching religion is that they assume religious organizations engage in that activity. But churches and other religious groups also object to the idea of teaching religion. They are suspicious of the word *religion* because it has general, objective, or academic connotations. Thus, the public school does not *teach* religion; the religious groups do not teach *religion*.

What I wish to do in this chapter is clarify the meanings of both *teach* and *religion*. After doing that I can proceed to describe in more detail the activity of teaching religion. The public school may have a peculiar idea of what it means to teach anything if it thinks that to teach religion is academically and constitutionally improper. Examining the teaching of religion may throw some light on the teaching of anything.

Religious bodies, I have said, are suspicious of religion, especially coming after the verb *to teach*. Nearly every religious group gives a prominent place to teaching, but what is to be taught is usually very restricted. One is not expected to teach religion but to teach the Word of God, Christian Doctrine, the way of the prophet, the catechism. A teacher may also be expected to teach by example, that is, he or she is to be a model of love, kindness, or the way.

A discussion of teaching in Christian churches will usually turn to the New Testament. Jesus of Nazareth is often referred to there as *the teacher.* Greek and Semitic notions of teaching were apparently similar: the teacher taught by giving example in a community. With the beginning of the church, however, the Christian movement had to face the same problem as have other religious groups, namely, after the teacher has departed how do the disciples pass on a way of life that has to be grasped largely through texts?

The solution to that dilemma is reflected in the way that New Testament literature used the word *teach.* The early church generally uses teaching as a follow-up to preaching. First one has to be converted on the occasion of announcing or preaching. (The deeper causes of conversion are another question.) When someone becomes a member of the assembly, he or she is ready for instruction in the details of the faith. Within this framework a teacher is one of the ministers of the church. Catholics as well as Protestants now refer to the "teaching ministry of the church."

The example of Jesus and the practice of the early church are relevant material for reflecting on the nature of teaching. But the academic field of religious education cannot directly appropriate New Testament language. Furthermore, while the New Testament has some fine material on the meaning of *to teach,* it has almost nothing to say about the teaching of religion. For many church people this fact is enough to prove that the teaching of religion is either innocuous or destructive. Before someone jumps to that conclusion it would be helpful to explore an alternate possibility, namely, that teaching religion cannot produce church members, but it may be useful and even necessary for church membership today.

In summary, the idea of teaching religion does not fit smoothly within either the public school or the religious organization. Possibly after the concept has been examined, the teaching of religion might still be considered peripheral to the interests of both institutions. My plea is simply that teaching religion be not *a priori* excluded from both institutions. If there is to be a field of religious education it has to find expression in the main educational and religious institutions of this society. The teaching of religion deserves examination as part of the field of religious education and in relation to educational and religious institutions.

The Teaching Act

What does it mean to teach something to somebody? This question has been investigated and debated in the West at least since the time of Plato. In Eastern religions a concern with teaching goes back much further. I make no pretensions to solve the issue once and for all. But I do think it is possible to insist upon a few distinctions that would open the issue of teaching religion in public school or in church/synagogue to more fruitful discussion.

First, I am assuming that religious education is a much larger issue than teaching religion. The description in chapter 2 of what is included in the whole field of religious education made little mention of the teaching of religion. I am presupposing that framework as I now turn to the meaning of *teach religion*. If church members say that religious education includes the practice of prayer, the example of parents, or actions for a just world, I can agree. I am also concerned that religious education include the teaching of religion as an important and neglected element.

Second, I am especially interested in *school* teaching as contrasted to other settings where one can use the verb *to teach*. Between the school and nonschool usage of the word *teach* there is continuity of meaning as well as some difference. I take the word *school* to refer mainly to literacy. Schooling is a form of education which depends upon learning to read and learning to read better. A school teacher cannot be judged successful unless students are able to understand the world through printed symbols.

To teach is to show someone how to do something. That is a common sense statement, but I think it is also the basis for scientific analysis. The act of teaching is a process that can be broken down into a series of steps. Some theories of teaching emphasize one or another of these steps. One person may see as most important what another views as secondary (e.g., the teacher's role in motivating the learner). If one concentrates on the act of teaching itself, rather than the teacher or the preconditions of the situation, the key issue is clearer. The act of teaching is captured in that wonderful Americanism, "know-how."

A teacher does not only know something but knows how to show the knowledge or skill to someone else. Sometimes the mastery of the teacher is obvious and expected. We are not surprised, for example, that Ted Williams could teach young baseball players to improve their hitting because Williams had extraordinary ability, training, and experience. But very often the best teachers in baseball are not the expert players. Perhaps their skill is in studying the best players and knowing how to explain things to less experienced players. An element of truth resides in the cynical adage: those who can, do; those who cannot, teach. A teacher of the violin may have "know-how" in training a student that the master violinist lacks.

Here is the source of the teacher's glory and humility: many of the learners will far outdistance the teacher.

I have referred above to baseball players and violinists as examples of teaching-learning. Reflection on teaching should begin with instances where the movement of the body is evident. School teaching has to be understood in relation to dealing with preverbal infants, music, sport, and all those situations where words are mainly choreography for the body. School teaching is a peculiar limit situation where the know-how turns back on the words themselves. Schools are places for teachers of words, a material that can be the richest of human resources or, when badly used, the thinnest of substances. Developmental psychology supports the traditional wisdom of not subjecting children to schooling before age five or six. Children begin acquiring language in the first year of life, but the language is for naming reality and for story-telling. School makes sense only when a child becomes reflectively self-conscious and can begin abstracting language from things.

The power to manipulate words and mathematical symbols does not arrive all at once. Teachers of the young know that history or algebra cannot be taught to eight-year-olds because these studies require a level of abstraction that comes later. Awareness of such conditions (whether derived from classroom experience or from reading Piaget) is part of the teacher's know-how. Most of schooling is directed at children who are still developing their conceptual powers. The strange thing is that our society seems to believe that school teaching should stop just when the power to school-learn is finally acquired.

This arrangement leads one to suspect that teaching is not the central concern of the schools that currently exist, or put differently, that teaching in schools is not primarily concerned with using the full range of verbal and conceptual powers. That suspicion is borne out by the history of the school teacher throughout the nineteenth and twentieth centuries. At the lower levels of education the teaching position has been one of nurturing; at the university level the job is usually called lecturing. These two ideas deserve some comment.

Teaching the young in this country has been assumed to be women's work. The prevalence of young women in the teaching profession is no accident. The nineteenth century was convinced of the perfect fit between being a woman and the profession of teaching. For Catherine Beecher, one of the most influential voices in this story, teaching was the natural extension of the "profession of womanhood." A woman's vocation was to mother or nurture the young. "Most happily, the education necessary to fit a woman to be a teacher, is exactly the one that best fits her for that domestic relation she is primarily designed to fill."[3]

The struggle between Horace Mann and the Boston schoolmasters in

1844 included the question of who would be the teachers. Mann's victory assured the dominance of "motherteacher."[4] Teachers were women and teaching was nurturing. Religion played a role in this shift of meaning for *teacher*. Patriarchal Puritanism was at that time being replaced by a softer, sentimental religiosity. The image of God as a stern and punishing taskmaster gave way to a kind, loving, and undemanding God.

The book published in the 1840s which stands at the crossroads of Protestant education is entitled *Christian Nurture*.[5] Horace Bushnell's masterpiece is still influential in religious circles today, and it is also important in the history of education. Bushnell wrote mainly about the family, where the word *nurture* obviously belongs. But he was not out of sympathy with Catherine Beecher's extension of the word *nurture* to teaching.

Bushnell's main concern was to offer an alternative to the revivalism of his day in which Protestant education was seen as preparation for conversion. He stressed the goodness and positive capacities of the child in opposition to the stern Protestantism that emphasized human depravity. Bushnell's work had a salutary effect on the church and especially the family, the main topic of *Christian Nurture*. Unfortunately, by lumping all the positive activity under the word *nurture*, Bushnell obscured the role of the school teacher. To this day teachers in church schools are described as people who nurture children in the faith. Bushnell's categories, *nurture* vs. *conversion*, still guide much of the discussion in church education. The autonomous activity of teaching does not appear at all. A teacher is not thought to be one who instructs, one who provokes the mind, one who searches after a truth that transcends all institutions.

At the university level one seldom hears discussion of the act of teaching. University professors have been predominantly men, and understandably they do not want to be classified as nurturers. Almost never would you hear a professor describe himself as a school teacher. Studies support this general impression. University professors identify themselves, not with the profession of education, but with their speciality of history, chemistry, or physics.[6]

Anyone who has been to a university can name good teachers he or she had. Very likely he or she can also make up a longer list of poor teachers. The sad fact is that whether the teaching is good or bad is largely an accident. Some people have native talent, an excellent speaking voice, or a flair for the dramatic. But teaching is seldom the major concern of the university; teaching is not consciously examined or cooperatively improved.

For lack of any other word to describe the university classroom, professors are said to *lecture*. Most of them in fact do not lecture, that is, they do not read to students. Professors in this country have seldom been comfortable bringing in a twenty-five-page written essay which can be read to a class in fifty minutes. The U.S. university is more casual and participatory than the word *lecture* suggests, although a residue of the form of lecturing is evident. What happens is often an awkward combination of lecturing, preaching, nurturing, and discussion.

Kenneth Eble, one of the few people studying university teaching, begins a chapter: "The best advice to the teacher who would lecture well is still: 'Don't lecture.' That is, for most of teaching to think in terms of discourse—talk, conversation—rather than lecture."[7] Eble does not take his own advice and goes on to write a chapter on lecturing. I think if he is intent on improving teaching—or even having teaching acknowledged as the work of the university—a more sustained attack upon the word *lecture* is needed. Substituting talk or conversation does nothing to change the basic form. Nor is what is needed more discussion groups in addition to lectures. What is needed is attention to the act of teaching as it occurs in everyday life.

In summary, teaching in the school setting ought not to forget its roots outside the school. Primary and secondary schools have to avoid letting teaching be absorbed by nurture; universities have to accept teaching as a responsibility distinct from scholarship. To teach is to show someone how to do something in such a way that it becomes part of the learner's experience. To school teach is to show how to use words and concepts to understand this world. The public school shies away from teaching religion because that sounds like nurturing in the faith. But to show someone how to use words and concepts for understanding religion is a responsibility of the schools. If the strengths and the limits of teaching are to be grasped by school teachers, they need to reflect on those who teach infants to dress themselves, those who teach illiterate adults to read, those who teach music, coach sports, or work with the handicapped.

Religion: An Academic Construct

My concern in this chapter is the teaching of religion. Having clarified the verb *to teach,* I now turn to the concept *religion.* As I discuss it here, *religion* is the direct object of the word *teach.* I am not interested in what someone might mean by "religious teaching." I do not deny that there are other questions about the religious element in education but here I focus on the word *religion.*

Religion is a concept that has built-in limitations. This fact gives it an innocuous or negative meaning to many Christian groups. In the specific setting of school teaching, those limitations might be an advantage.

Religion appears to be a general idea applicable to a set of things called religions. But nearly all Christian, Jewish, Muslim, Buddhist, or Hindu groups would protest against their way of life being classified as one religion among others. The internal language of each of those groups contains distinctions between "we the people who are specially designated by God" and "everyone else." Other people have religion; we have the faith (the truth, God's Word, the revelation, the way).

As I indicated in chapter 3 there is an almost universal assumption in the modern world that this internal language of religious traditions is wrong and intolerant. The simple solution of modern scholarship is to eliminate the claims to chosen people or uniqueness; and then religion is a neatly scientific category. The protest of Christian, Jewish, Buddhist, or Muslim devotees is that such an idea of religion destroys what they consider most important in their way of life. This situation reveals the importance of teaching religion; that is, it would be the setting in which to examine the conflicting claims of traditional groups and modern scholars.

Religion is a word that goes back to pre-Christian history, but its usual meaning today dates only from the eighteenth and nineteenth centuries. In both ancient and modern meanings, *religion* is one of the few words that has a chance of mediating Christian, Jewish, Orthodox, Muslim, and Hindu differences. In its ancient meaning, *religio* referred to the bond between God and the human manifested in attitude and behavior. The Christian church with its final answer to human longing saw itself pitted against the devotion (or religion) of the pagans. In time, the church took over many of the pre-Christian concepts, integrating them into its final solution. Some people view this process as a corruption, and undoubtedly there has been corruption, but it is difficult to imagine how the Christian movement could have avoided the absorption of non-Christian concepts. By the time of St. Augustine it was possible to write a treatise, *De Vera Religione,* referring to the genuine piety of Christians.

In the twentieth century we might assume that the title of Augustine's work means: Christianity is the one true religion among all the religions of the world. That idea is a modern thesis conceivable only after the invention of religion in scholarly circles. That is, our common understanding of religion as an object that can stand next to psychology or politics is a quite recent idea.

Is the modern idea of religion, as many conservative Christian groups maintain, an abomination applicable only to one's opponents? The distrust of this idea is understandable, but the total disjunction of Christianity and religion simply avoids facing up to an issue that will not go away. The existence of the modern concept of religion is evidence that there are a number of groups in the world who claim to be the true way. The two possibilities we now have to choose between are: (1) a respectful and growing understanding of the similarities and differences among major religious traditions; this means an education in religious matters including the teaching of religion; or (2) the union of religious groups is given over to scientists with a rationalistic bent; when that does not work, as it almost certainly will not, the job will be left to politicians and generals.

Religion, it is sometimes said, does not belong in school. My claim, based partly on the origin of its modern meaning, is that school is precisely where religion belongs. It is an academic category which should not be casually thrown about anywhere but which can be an instrument of understanding in the world of books. Religion, like history, is not the name of an object; it is an idea and a method posited by scholars. It represents a commitment to use the mind in a search for truth. That can be dangerous, I have admitted, but it is more dangerous in the modern world to isolate oneself from modern inquiry into historical, scientific, and philosophical truth.

Religion is not what one lives. People follow the words of the prophet or live in Christ or become Bodhisatvas. None of these ideals can simply be reduced to a general classification of religion. But, for example, the meaning of "to live in Christ" might be developed by relating this ideal not only to the literature of the whole Bible but to other religious and nonreligious ideals. This process of inquiry, despite the possible misunderstandings, deserves to be called "the study and teaching of religion."

A "scientific study of religion" grew up in the environment of nineteenth-century rationalism and in reaction to Christian theology. This problem of origins has not been entirely surmounted. Christian scholars shift between wanting to take over the word *religion* and rejecting it entirely. We need a setting in which to work out the tensions between *Christian* and *religious*. Some bias against Christian tradition would be revealed but also some bias against non-Christian peoples.

The popular notion of modern science is not very hospitable to the peculiar practices and insistent commitments of religious people. Ian Barbour notes that if you think of religion as "articles of faith" and science as "tentative hypotheses," then there is unresolvable conflict between science and religion. But if what exists historically are religious traditions on one side and research traditions of science on the other side, a fruitful dialogue becomes possible.[8] Then one can teach religion just as one can teach physics while respecting the distinctive natures of the religious tradition and the research tradition of science. Religion signifies the willingness to use the mind to understand one's own religious tradition and that of other peoples.

The Teaching of Religion

Having separately analyzed the concepts of *teach* and *religion,* I return to my original question: "What does it mean to teach religion?" I have narrowed the question from both sides. The question is neither "What does it mean to educate people in religious matters?" (which includes more than teaching), nor "What does it mean to teach a person to act religiously?" (which includes more than religion). Rather, I am asking "What does it mean to show a person how to use words and concepts so as to understand a field called religion?"

The assumption I begin with is that there are activities and texts which are generally regarded as religious. Although there would be debates about whether to include some material, especially recent documents, the main religious traditions of the human race are fairly easy to identify. It would be unwise to exclude all modern documents, but in establishing the existence of a field of religion it is easier to start with the Qu'ran, the Bhagavad Gita, or the Bible.

A first aim in teaching religion is to make the material intelligible, or more minimally stated, to show that the material is not unintelligible. A teacher can make some sense of what religious people do and can correlate the behavior with their verbal expressions. Concerning some contemporary movements there may be little sense to make; that is, close examination of a group may lead the student to the conviction that it is a fraud. But for any tradition that has lasted hundreds or thousands of years, one has to be cautious about drawing any final conclusions, especially the judgment that such a tradition is false or irrational.

A teacher can do no more than make partially intelligible the language of a religious tradition. Because religious language (or language used for a religious purpose) has a peculiar character, the teacher can only claim to have understood its meaning up to a point. Religious systems do not claim to explain the world completely, but they do claim to give a more comprehensive meaning to experience than any other systems. Religious documents can only be understood by someone willing to approach the texts with reverence, sympathy, and a willingness to see the entire picture conveyed by the documents.

The categories that have confused discussion in this area are *subjective vs. objective* and a parallel contrast of *believer vs. unbeliever.* Though there may be some limited usefulness to these concepts, their functioning as the framework of discussion obstructs understanding. *Subjective/objective* is an inappropriate instrument for describing the teaching of religion. Both the words *teach* and *religion* connote objectivity. "Objective teaching" and "teaching objective religion" are redundant phrases. On the other hand, there is no teaching without subjective involvement of a teacher, and there is no understanding of religion except through the subjective realm of religious people.

The appropriate framework is to view a religious text as a mediator between a community of the past and a community of the present. The school teacher's job is to see that the text has a chance to fulfill this role. Teaching religion is a case of "disciplined intersubjectivity."[9] A community (subjects) shares its insights with another community through the disciplined use of symbols (objects). The teacher has to be the most disciplined in trying to determine the meaning of what was said in the context of another era. The chief criteria of this disciplined intersubjectivity are fairness and fullness.

Does one not need "faith" to understand the Bible or the Qu'ran? If the word *faith* could be used with all of its meaning it might be a helpful term here. One would have to distinguish among "believing in" as a fundamental attitude of trust, "belief" as an act of the mind, and "beliefs" as convictions held to be true. All three meanings can be developed in relation to diverse religious traditions. So long as writers say *believer* and *unbeliever* when they really mean *Christian* and *not Christian* then the role of faith in studying religion cannot be clarified.

For the understanding of religious meaning one has to participate in the meaning to some degree. The teacher has to be able to put himself or herself in the shoes of the writer and see the world from that perspective. Can anyone really do that? The answer would seem to be: Yes, up to a point. A white person cannot see the world from an identical perspective with a black. A man cannot see the world exactly as a woman. But our common humanity allows for some degree of participation. Can a Catholic understand a Lutheran text? Can a Republican understand Democratic policies? Religion and politics have some similarity here. To understand politics one has to participate in political life in some way. It is not necessary to belong to one of the major parties to understand politics; and if a person belongs to one party, it does not prevent his or her understanding the other party.

What then would be the difference in a course on religion in a public school and in a school under religious auspices? To be specific, what difference is there between teaching St. Mark's Gospel in PS 109 and in St. Mary's School?

The answer at the level of principle is that there will probably be more contextual meaning available in St. Mary's School. In the church school it might be assumed that students are already living in a way that embodies some of the meaning of the Gospel. They have some familiarity with the Gospel through exposure to parents, teachers, and symbols in their immediate environment. There should not be contradiction between what is taught in the two schools though there is room for difference in emphasis.

The above contrast is made at the level of general principle. In practice, the question of context gets extremely complex. Suppose a student at St. Mary's for one of a variety of reasons does not want to study St. Mark's Gospel. That factor may invalidate all the positive possibilities in the environment. Or suppose that the environment of St. Mary's is in a sense overrich in religious meaning. Too much of one kind of religious symbolism too early may make the high school student resistant to religion. The public school with a diversity of religious meanings and a nonreligious context might actually be a more fruitful setting to study St. Mark's Gospel in depth. The crucial element is the discipline of the teacher. Does the teacher in the church school really attend to the text when there is no challenge of diverse religious positions? Does the teacher in the public school have the skill to judge fairly between differing positions? The academic, institutional, and political difficulties of teaching religion are great, but the direction in which to move is clear.

In a school, whether public or religiously affiliated, the main attention has to be on symbols, practices, and documents. That is not to say that the teaching of religion and the teaching of mathematics occur in identical form. The material of religion lends itself to a more personal involvement. The teacher draws upon the meaning of the environment which includes the experience of students and teachers. How much of the student's inner life comes into direct focus should depend upon the freedom of the student.

In his study of religious experience, Edward Robinson found that people seldom bring up their most personal and profound religious experience in school.[10] This fact is a bad symptom of how people feel about school. I would still insist that the school teacher's main attention has to be symbols and text. If the setting is reverent and nonthreatening, the student will perhaps volunteer some of his or her private experience for discussion. If the student does not, there may be a failing on the teacher's part, but it may also be that the appropriate time and place have not yet arrived.

Religious groups often cannot see the necessity and value of teaching religion with the discipline and limitations I have indicated. They may wish the successful result (e.g., knowledge of the Bible) without the patience and the risk that are its conditions. Church schools are often unsuccessful because they do not wish to waste the time of truly being a school where literature is appreciated and a variety of religious literature is explored. There cannot be a Christian education without a religious education; Bible teaching presupposes book learning.

As the neo-orthodox reaction in Protestant education replaced the religious education movement in the 1950s, James Smart castigated those writers who were not truly *Christian* educators because they did not have Jesus Christ at the center.[11] He does not consider the possibility that religious education, in addition to "the teaching ministry of the church," might be a help in building a bridge to the public school (which he treats in chapter 10) and might even be a help to Christian students in their church school. At one point, Smart notes: "Curiously, children treated under the second type of program, in which the Bible is not central, often come away with a better knowledge of the Bible than those who have been permitted to study nothing but the Bible."[12] I don't think it is curious at all. Those who "have been permitted to study nothing but the Bible" obviously will lack a sense of literature and be unable to appreciate the literary and historical scholarship that illuminates the Bible today.

In the past, religious bodies have often been accused of substituting indoctrination for teaching and sentimentality for scholarship. Teaching religion, especially in the context of the public school, has to avoid these deficiencies. When we react against the past, however, it is important to get the contrasts well stated. An English writer says: "In the religious education of the seventies the ability to teach the subject no longer depends on the teacher's own convictions. He may be a Christian, he may belong to one of the other faiths, he may be a humanist. Or he may himself be searching and so not come into any of these categories."[13] The direction the English writer wishes to go may be discernible, but all three sentences state the case badly. Surely the convictions of a teacher are crucial, especially convictions about the nature of religion and the rules of fairness. "Christian, one of the other faiths, humanist" is an illogical set of choices. And "searching" would seem to be an always desirable characteristic for teachers and religious people.

The question for the future is whether we can find ordinary teachers in sufficient numbers who can carry out the work of teaching religion in a responsible way. There will probably never be vast numbers of teachers who can knowledgeably comment on all the religious positions in the world. What we can realistically hope for is intelligent participants in religious life who grow in their skill as teachers. Religion is an academic construct. A teacher does not have to have mastered all of its intricacies before he or she starts to teach. The teacher just has to arrive at the point of being able to show someone that a religious life is not unintelligible and that while the teacher is deeply convinced of the value of his or her own position it is possible to respect and in part to understand other positions.

The way in which I have been describing the teaching of religion does not assume that the students are children. Schooling is a form of learning that we require of the young, and on the whole the requirement is a wise one. Today, however, schooling is appropriate for people of any age. To the study of religion adults can bring a richness of personal context and a developed sense of fairness. A person at seventy or eighty years of age may finally be ready to confront the great religious texts with simplicity of outlook and a tolerance of diversity. Religious officials often seem unaware that many older people are in search of solid substance for the mind. The number who want intellectually challenging study in the area of religion is almost certain to increase in the coming decades. Public institutions of learning as well as religiously affiliated schools are not yet doing the teaching job in religion that needs to be done.

6
Work and Leisure
Within Religious Education

The field of religious education has to include, besides schooling, other areas of learning. As I pointed out at the end of the last chapter, schooling is not or should not be reserved exclusively for children. The church and the university ought to be offering challenging courses on the Bible, church history, the Talmud, theology, and so on. Nonetheless, for the majority of adults school will probably occupy only a small part of their time. What more often engage their attention are questions of work and leisure. An educational model that excludes work and leisure cannot reach adults in their adult lives. The field of religious education should be especially concerned with the issues of work and leisure.

The person who is designated "religious educator" in a parish may feel unqualified to deal with topics raised in this chapter. That is not surprising; none of us can be experts on all these matters. Two points are helpful to keep in mind: (1) No one person is responsible for all of the religious education of others. That fact might relieve some anxieties about a failure to do the whole job; it might also get teachers to recognize new allies. (2) The teacher who cannot pretend to be competent in all aspects of work and leisure might play the role of catalyst; the experiences of other people in the church or synagogue might be drawn upon so that religious education becomes more of a team effort. As I note in chapter 10, many middle-aged men, precisely in the work side of their lives, are an untapped resource for religious education.

Numerous articles and books appear each month on work and leisure in the United States.[1] The word *problem* shows up in this literature not only in the discussion of jobs but also in the use of leisure time; the nature of the problem, however, is difficult to identify. Paradoxes abound: while some women are fighting to get into the job market, many women would like nothing better than to get out of it; some people are working to raise the retirement age, while in many places the retirement age is being lowered; leisure time is rapidly increasing for nearly everyone, but many people feel they have no leisure at all in their lives.

I would suggest that the paradoxes surrounding the work/leisure issue lead us into the area of religion. Educational programs that try to solve the problems of work and leisure eventually get into questions that are religious in nature. Our past religious traditions and some elements in current church structure have something to offer in the present discussion of work and leisure. Thus, work/leisure is central to the defining of religious education and, in turn, religious education can be an interpretive key to work/leisure.

In the relation of work/leisure to education, a preliminary distinction is necessary: there is education *to* work and education *by* work. That is, our society prepares people for their jobs, and, far from being neglected, this part of education may be overstressed. We educate people to become engineers, businessmen, teachers, and so forth, but there is also education in the doing of jobs, and here education is often deficient. What does an assembly line do to a person, and how could we better organize the job? What does bureaucracy continuously teach people in government and business? An attentiveness to what the job itself teaches might change the way we prepare people for working at jobs.

The distinction between an education *to* and an education *by* also applies to leisure. We now have programs that prepare people for retirement. In addition, adult education programs have traditionally offered people help in the use of their leisure time. What would education *by* leisure mean? If you go mountain climbing during your summer vacation that presumably teaches you something. But what about people who are retired or are outside the job market? Could there be any educational value in doing nothing? This part of the issue suggests the need for some finer distinctions, which will lead us into historical and religious questions.

I would like to propose here two distinctions: that between job and work; that between leisure as free time and leisure as contemplation. These two distinctions are rooted in religious history, and they also have some currency in contemporary speech. Job and free time are part of the ordinary fare of life; work and contemplation are a call to something better than our usual routines. These distinctions are religious if one means by religious the attempt to affirm what is greater than the ordinary. A religiously educational approach is to affirm what is more than ordinary while not denying the ordinary or undercutting its value.

I conclude from the above that one way to define religious education would be that it is anything which affirms and improves our jobs but at the same time reminds us that we have work to do. For some poor jobs the best that can immediately be done is to lessen the burden of them. But even the best of jobs is no more than a partial embodiment of the calling God gives us to contribute our work to the transformation of the world. Similarly, religious education can be described as a concern that people have free time, but with the awareness that our lives move toward the still point at the center of the universe. People are not free merely by being off the job but by the gradual integration of active and receptive modes of living. In this use of language, job and free time are mutually exclusive realities whereas work and contemplation imply one another.

Historical Note

Before I describe work, leisure, and an educational response to each, an historical note will be helpful as background. The Hebrew Bible does not have much to say about work, but it gets to the point quickly. In Genesis, Adam is placed in a garden where he is to till the soil, name the animals, and fill the earth. The sin of Adam brings the penalty of laboring "in the sweat of your brow." Work, in this view, is part of the human condition— natural, enjoyable, and fruitful—and yet is also caught in the drudgery that accompanies human sinfulness.

The Hebrew Bible doesn't return much to this question. In the pessimistic view of Ecclesiastes, work seems to be a vanity and an "unhappy business." But the outlook of Genesis is never rescinded. In contrast to Sumerian and Babylonian myths of creation, humans are not created to take over drudgery from the gods. In the Jewish story humans are partners with God in the whole work of creation.

A few direct things about work are said in the New Testament, but these texts need a context. The Gospels portray Jesus as the son of a carpenter, perhaps implying that he did some carpentering too. But the Gospels do not show Jesus on the job from nine to five. They do describe him being "about his Father's business" day and night. While engaged in his peculiar kind of business or work, he also withdraws on occasion for periods of quiet and prayer.

Two texts of St. Paul refer to work, but they cannot easily be made into a Christian doctrine of work. In both passages Paul is speaking about the missionary and his right to receive support from the community. Paul is proud that his job as tentmaker enables him to be a self-supporting missionary. He nonetheless insists that the missionary should be supported.

One line of St. Paul has been quoted repeatedly in Western history: "If anyone will not work, let him not eat." It has been used as a condemnation of welfare legislation in the United States and England. It is even used (without acknowledgement of its source) in the 1936 Constitution of the Soviet Union. St. Paul is restating here a principle found throughout the Bible: that work is a good in human life. The text cannot be used indiscriminately to set policy regarding the very young, the very old, the disabled, and the unfortunate.

In Western history before the modern era, people had what we now call jobs and they also had time off. The word *job* is fairly recent, but a word with some similar connotations that does fit the preindustrial world is *labor*. People have labored all through the centuries doing what was necessary to feed, clothe, and shelter themselves.

Human beings also need respite from their labors; they take time each day for eating, sleeping, and recreation. On a periodic basis they take part of a week or a year as time for rest. Judaism has the practice of the Sabbath, which the Christian church adopted and modified. By the time of the Middle Ages there were dozens of holydays on which, along with the Christian Sabbath, one did no "servile work." According to Aquinas, labor was a necessity for the human race, but that is not to say either that everyone should labor or that anyone should labor as much as possible.

The Protestant Reformers wished to lessen the distance between peoples' ordinary labors and the religious meaning of their lives. The Reformation brought back to prominence the eschatological element, that is, an emphasis on the end time. There is no time to waste as our ordinary lives converge with God's calling us to salvation in Christ.

For both Luther and Calvin, the word *work* along with *vocation* and *calling* needed freeing from the monastery and people whose lives did not seem very productive. From now on the religious lives of the saints could be lived outside the monastic walls. "No task will be sordid and base, provided you obey your calling in it."[2]

The lessening of the distance between ordinary labor and vocational • work meant that one's job in the new order was a good thing. The other side of this emphasis on the job as good was the implication that not having a job is bad. Obviously, one couldn't always be on the job, but time away from the job became suspect if not evil. The opposite of job was not leisure but idleness, and no saying is better known in the United States than "an idle mind is the devil's workshop."

Today, of course, there must be an abundance of workshops from which the devil can choose. Idleness, which was renamed *leisure time* in the nineteenth century, has increased at an astounding rate. The current estimate is that on the average a person has twenty-two years more of leisure than a century ago. An increase of leisure time is thought to be desirable, but what is one to do with twenty-two years of undefined space? Recognizing that the issue of job and free time raises questions unanswerable by an economist, John Maynard Keynes wrote: "There is no country and no people who can look forward to the age of leisure and abundance without a dread."[3] Part of the answer might be to go back into classical and early Christian history to rethink the relation of work and leisure. At the same time we may find groups in the present who have preserved the premodern meanings of work and leisure.

Work

In the definition of Thomas Green, "work is that activity by which men [and women] refuse to acknowledge that life is vain."[4] *Job* on the other hand, is a modern concept that refers to something partial and something for which you usually get paid. In a culture that lessened the distance from job to work but lost the eschatological impulse of the Reformers, work is liable to be swallowed by job. We let the Department of Labor define work for us, and then what is not paid employment can easily become not work but drudgery. We assign most jobs to males between ages sixteen and sixty-five and think that is the extent of work. We can begin to address this problem by always distinguishing between *job* and *work*. This distinction includes appreciating and naming as work what has not been and may never be paid employment.

The forms of work that are not usually jobs are evident in the lives of children, youth, the aged, and women. The need, therefore, is twofold: (1) The word *work* must be extended to these groups, a project which will be helped by also opening up some jobs to them. (2) The world of jobs should be changed as it becomes open to children, youth, the aged, and more women.

1) **Children.** No one familiar with the history of childhood would be nostalgic about the time when children were thrown into the middle of the laborious struggle for survival. Nor does the early Industrial Era and its exploitation of child labor provide any model for us. The child labor laws, beginning in 1836, represented real progress. But exploiting child labor and letting children be in the middle of work are not the same thing. Children today to their own disadvantage seldom see adults working at jobs. Simply mixing children into the job site could be a help to children; even better would be finding jobs that might allow children some economic independence.

The immediate objection is that offices and factories are not designed for children. While that is true, one can draw an opposite conclusion from the one usually drawn. We should redesign many job sites so that they would be better adapted to children. That move, I am suggesting, would help the job to become more like work for the adults. Conceptions of factory and office are often left over from an early industrial era. As technology becomes miniaturized and as most products become plastic, our huge factories and assembly lines are of questionable value. As jobs become more mental than physical, the very idea of office/factory may become outdated.

Children can awaken us to these facts because a child's work is play. Probably most jobs in the modern world would be better "played at" then "labored at." Great scientists always remind us that their discoveries come from playing with their knowledge. The service part of the economy is also a playing at a role. Those who know how to play may not get their lives fulfilled as waitresses, bank tellers, or secretaries, but the job is more bearable and they may have some energy left for the off-the-job activities which may be their real work.

Children don't have to be taught to play, but they can be helped to play better. Play includes discipline, training, and access to material resources. Girls as well as boys should have all the advantages of physical training and participation in team sports. Play and athletics are central to the religious education of children. Play could also have a major part in helping adults to distinguish job and work, allowing them to take the job seriously but not to become obsessed with it. Childlike play might redirect some of the destructive gamesmanship that already exists in high executive positions.

2) **Youth.** Young people even more obviously than children need mixing into the world of jobs. Here there exists a base on which to build. Three-fourths of college students are already engaged in employed work. That statistic might surprise some college professors and educational theorists who define youth as a time before work. The community college system, where the average age is about twenty-seven, has altered the meaning of college student. This development needs building upon and improvement. Students need better combinations of work (i.e., job)/study. If possible, the job should be an apprenticeship in the field which they are studying.

School should be experienced as real work by young people. If school is simply a place for certification for jobs, then school becomes laborious drudgery. Young people then feel that their labor is being exploited without pay. School ought to be a place for hard work but not hard labor. School as work includes playing with knowledge and being receptive to ancient wisdom.

In turn the world of the job would change if there were more contact with young people and with schools. In the present and increasingly in the future, one job may not be enough for a lifetime. People have to be learning on the job so that they can do the old job in new ways. Quite possibly they will also come to the point of needing a new job. Young people and schools could keep alive an experimental attitude and an adventurous spirit in the area of job.

3) **The Old.** For most people there comes a time to retire from the labor force, but this must not be confused with retiring from work. The presence of old people can give a different attitude to employed workers. The old are a reminder that whether I am twenty-five or fifty-five I had better not equate my life with my job. One can make a valuable contribution to this world whether or not one is paid. However, this contribution from the old presupposes that society remove an intolerable financial burden on many old people and also make jobs available to those who want them.

The argument over whether to have a retirement age, and what that age should be, seldom gets precise enough. Some jobs may be better done by the young and others better done by the old. In some jobs age doesn't matter. We need social approbation for all forms of work and also an intelligent distribution of paid employment. Older people who have less physical energy but greater human wisdom may hold a key to our grasping what work means. We still need productive labor in the twentieth century, but we also need the work of wisdom and holiness.

4) **Women.** Great numbers of poor women have always been in the labor market. They have not had much leverage to change the system of jobs. The entrance of another class of women into the labor force could dramatically change jobs and work for everyone. The danger is that more women might get jobs, but the relation of job to work would not change much. What happens to job/work in the future depends largely on two tasks that have been generally assigned to women: childcare and housework.

Childcare, it could be plausibly argued, is the most important work in the world. But often it is not thought to be work at all because of our tendency to equate work and job. In the government's *Dictionary of Occupational Titles,* "childcare attendant" ranked 878th in importance, at the same level as parking lot attendant but behind dog pound attendant.[5] Feminist groups have forced a change in the ranking, but advancing childcare up the ranks doesn't establish the fact that childcare is invaluable work, whether or not it is a job at all.

My point is not to argue against the extension of childcare centers. I am assuming that this development is an urgent necessity. But to be both economically feasible and humanly successful, childcare has to be placed in this context of job and work. Childcare centers don't fit our present system of jobs and our conception of who is a worker. The argument for childcare centers cannot simply be that the government should provide more dollars so that more women can get jobs. Adequate childcare requires us to rethink the relationships of women and men, young and old, home and job site, family and nonfamilial groups. While still fighting for more money, advocates of childcare centers must devise new forms of cooperation between families, design nonbureaucratic organizations, and involve people defined as unemployable (e.g., people classified as retired or as retarded).

Housework is my final litmus test of whether we are really changing our job and work arrangements. The example may appear trivial, but this question is primordial. Housework shows in microcosm all of the modern problems of job and work. Like childcare, part of it can be made into a paying job, but it will likely remain a nonpaying form of work as well. My suggestions for a religiously educational approach to housework are quite simple: (1) What is laborious drudgery should be reduced by technology; however, there is a point (already passed in many U.S. households) where more gadgets get in the way and are ecologically indefensible. (2) The inevitable residue of labor should be shared equally and here I mean exact equality. Men and women, rich and poor, fastidious intellectuals, should all take their share in caring for the home. (3) Other aspects of homemaking, when freed from the drudgery, can be creative work. Choosing plants, decorating walls, or cooking food can be pleasurable and open to all. Creative work may require some preparation. For example, boys as well as girls should be taught to cook so that everyone can share in both the pleasurable work and the accompanying labor of preparing meals.

Leisure

In turning now to leisure I am addressing the same question as above but from a different angle. The word *leisure* is a further challenge to our assumptions about work. If work is to change then so too must leisure. One of the first needs here is to rediscover the earlier meaning of leisure which has been swamped by our use of *leisure* as meaning free time. Churches can exercise considerable influence here. Leisure as contemplation may seem alien to our culture, but that doesn't mean people won't respond to it if they could experience it. The question is whether religious educators themselves see contemplation as a practical concern at the heart of religious education.

For reasons discussed above there was little concern with leisure in the United States until the late nineteenth century. In fact, the concept can hardly be said to have existed. There was plenty of writing on the virtues of discipline, thrift, and devotion to one's calling. Toward the end of the last century "the word idleness crawls out of its ugly cocoon to turn into a beautiful butterfly—leisure."[6] The economic system demanded that people have more time off so that they could consume goods. Those who didn't have jobs became the "unemployed," a concept born in the same period as "leisure time."[7] To have leisure time seemed desirable, and to be unemployed undesirable, but both take their meaning from having a job.

What the twentieth century seems to demand is that half of life be disciplined, rational, and productive while the other half be undisciplined, irrational, and consumerist. Not surprisingly, some people get confused: they are lazy on the job or they labor at their free time or, most ironically, they get the two areas reversed—unproductive on the job and harried in their leisure time. U.S. society appears to many people as schizoid in this division and confusion.

The way out of the dilemma requires a reappropriation and reinstitution of the classical meaning of *leisure.* I have indicated this meaning with the word *contemplation.* This term may not carry the intended connotations to some people, but I am trying to describe an attitude of peace, wholeness, and centeredness. The philosophical act is contemplative and so is religious worship. Looking at the ocean can be contemplative and sitting quietly with a friend can be too. A contemplative person is at rest not outside the world but at its center.

The objection to this classical meaning of *leisure* has been that it is founded on a society of two classes: free men and slaves. A minority could afford leisure because the necessities of life were taken care of by servants and women. Widespread technology, however, changes these possibilities—for better or worse. The machine can reduce labor so that more and more people get a taste of contemplative leisure. However, technology only provides the possibility. Also needed are efficient democracy, distribution of wealth, good education, and religious reverence. Otherwise, leisure as contemplation is available only for a very few, while leisure as unfilled time is what the masses are given.

The groups I have discussed above who were excluded from the job market have preserved elements of the contemplative attitude. The play of children embodies one aspect of contemplative leisure. Young people who are in school (the Greek word for *leisure*) can remind us of another meaning of leisure. Women who have cared for children and cared for the home have had to develop a contemplative attitude toward a form of work that is an endless cycle of labor, but outside the labor market. Finally, old people who have "retired" can remind us that we all need a sense of detachment while trying to do our jobs well.

The leisure attitude is possible on the job and off the job. It is available for those who labor with their hands and those whose jobs are mostly mental. Nonetheless, conditions can either encourage or discourage the development of this attitude. A sense of peace in the home and an aesthetically pleasing school certainly help. The job site needs to be free from dehumanizing noise, dirt, and conflict. In short, everyone has to look for places and times of quiet that cultivate a contemplative attitude. To those conditions one might wish to add techniques of meditation, but such techniques are effective only in the right environment.

Conclusions for Churches

From the above reflections on work and leisure I would like to draw some conclusions for church and religious education.

1) **Work.** There is an evident need to continue the fight for reform of the industrial order. The struggle includes efforts to reduce unfair discrimination against minority groups and women. Some people need jobs, and other people need access to better jobs. For some people their jobs can be their primary work; for other people their work can be in addition to job. Churches are institutions that can both pressure to improve jobs and give people the opportunity to participate in work which isn't a job.

One of the worst usages in contemporary American English is *vocational education.* Since the turn of the century the rich have had careers while the poor have had vocations. John Dewey spoke of "vocational aspects of education" for everyone; that meaning is already a reduction in the rich meaning of the word *vocation,* but at least the word referred to everyone.[8] The most preferable religious usage would be to say that each of us has a vocation in this world, and sometimes it is expressed in our jobs. People who write books, teach school, or preach in church have rather pleasant vocational jobs. Poor people have a difficult enough time without their being constantly told that their jobs are "vocational." It is precisely the poor whose jobs often do very little to express their vocations in life. Religious educators should be in the forefront of changing the language of vocational education.

Another area that I emphasized as needing better naming is childcare. Churches and schools can make an impact here both in the way they speak of childcare and in the provision of some services. The parish or local church can be a coordinator or at least a place for meetings across family lines. Occasional help for a busy mother can make the difference between childcare as a laborious burden and childcare as hard but enjoyable work. In any case, religious educators should be most resistant to that language which inquires of a woman whether she works or is a housewife.

2) **Leisure.** Churches have an historic mission today to be zones of quiet. I hope it is evident by this point that quiet, far from being escapist, is at the center of political action. A church, school, or retreat center is not a place to step out of the world but to withdraw into the middle of the world.

This symbol of center raises a question about the location of most retreat houses. I do think more of them ought to be in the middle of cities rather than in rural areas, though I am not denying the value of the latter. Going to a desert or the top of a mountain can be a helpful activity in education, but the test of contemplation is the hollowing out of a sphere of silence within the noise of the ordinary world. Churches and education centers can be places for developing this attitude.

Besides the need for place there is also a need for time—each day, each week, each year. Many Catholics have the practice of annual retreats, and many Protestant churches have the tradition of vacation schools. The weekly day of rest was maintained in the United States until recently. Now there seems to be an unsuccessful effort to continue the closing of stores on Sunday. We may be losing that wonderful sense of Sabbath which Christians took over from Jews. "We usually think that the earth is our mother, that time is money and profit our mate. The seventh day is a reminder that God is our father, that time is life and the spirit our mate."[9] The reference to the seventh day here recalls us to the fact that Jews and Christians have never agreed on what day is to be celebrated this way.

For the first time in our history it may now be realistic for Christians and Jews to join in the attempt to sanctify the weekend. While some stores and other services have to continue on Saturday and Sunday, nearly everyone in our society should be able to get some free time on the weekend to celebrate the Sabbath. The Catholic church's Saturday service furthers a bond with Judaism. What has been a sore point of conflict could now be ameliorated if not eliminated. Fighting a rear guard action to protect Sunday is no longer the way to view the question. Christians and Jews have a common interest in trying to provide the Sabbath experience for everyone—for most on Saturday or Sunday or, if not then, on another day.

3) **Work and Leisure.** The church service itself can be a demonstration of the union of work and leisure. A liturgical ceremony can be a skilled and disciplined work. At the same time it can be peacefully contemplative. A test of celebration is whether it has generous amounts of quiet at its center. A worshiping community is one that provides us with a solitude that is different from loneliness. Such a community allows us to confront the aloneness that is part of the human condition without being destroyed by it.

Art and play are integral to divine worship because in each of these activities a carefully controlled ritual embodies a contemplative attitude. Churches should be places for the arts and for sports. Granted, these two activities can be either escapism for the comfortable, or exploitation of the poor. But with all their potential for corruption, art and sport root us in the ordinary flow of life even while reminding us that there is a greater realm to come "where all that is not music will be silence."

7
Professionalizing
Religious Education

Religious education is the name of both an academic field and a profession. In the preceding chapters I have been describing some of the elements that make up the field of study. An understanding of the field of religious education requires acquaintance with the literature of education as well as material on the nature and practice of religion. In this chapter I turn to the other side of the issue and ask about the possibilities of a *profession* called *religious education.* Although the topic draws upon some of the same literature as the academic field, a different framework and an additional body of literature have to be introduced. As I said in chapter 2, a field is a necessary but not sufficient condition for the existence of a profession. The concept of profession itself needs clarifying, and then the idea of a profession of religious education has to be investigated.

Who wishes to be called *unprofessional?* Not many people, I would guess, judging from the extensive literature on professionalization. We sometimes seem to be moving toward "the professionalization of everyone."[1] The desire to be a professional seems especially strong these days among parish religious educators in the Roman Catholic church. I have no intention of attacking the trend toward professionalization, but I think that the ideas of *professional* and *profession* need closer examination than they usually receive in church circles. We need in the first place an historical perspective on the somewhat mysterious concept of profession. The history of the professional is only now being written, but several excellent studies have appeared in recent years.[2]

The historical sketch at the beginning of this chapter will throw light on the fact that two professions, indeed two *kinds* of profession, exist in churches today. This situation is the cause of considerable confusion, but it could also be the source of a new burst of vitality. The parish director of religious education (or coordinator) in the Catholic church is at a crucial spot in the shifting form of church organization. The emergence of this new professional could be one of the most important things to have happened in the Catholic church since Vatican II, but this new structure is extremely fragile. Few individuals survive for very long as DRE/coordinator and unless further clarification and change are forthcoming the future of this profession is not promising.[3] Although I am concentrating in this chapter on the Roman Catholic church as the concrete example, with minor changes these considerations are applicable to other churches, and with further changes they could also apply to religious groups that are not Christian.

A recent study from an official source in the Catholic church is called *A National Inventory of Parish Catechetical Programs*.[4] This study could be depressing to anyone advocating professionalization. Two examples of the study's data will indicate why: (1) Only 7 percent of parish directors earn $10,000 or more; 49 percent are unpaid. (2) One-third of directors do not have a college degree. The *Inventory* makes an unfortunate choice of terms that confuses the meaning of such figures: it describes as *DRE* anyone said to be in charge of the parish's education. There is no clear logic to this terminology given that only 32 percent described themselves this way. Fifty-one percent of the people surveyed called themselves "coordinator" and 9 percent called themselves "the pastor." The result is that *DRE*, the most likely term to indicate some specific professional characteristics, is rendered almost meaningless by its indiscriminate application.

The *Inventory's* picture can look so bleak that one is forced to ask: Is the Catholic church on some other path than that of modern professionalization, and, if so, is that all bad? The question is not meant to allow excuses for low salaries and incompetent work in the church. Rather, the reason for the question is to probe whether the modern meaning of *professional* is an unambiguous good. Possibly some of what is assumed to be a weakness of the church can from another perspective be seen as a strength. What is called *under-professionalization* might actually be a premodern form of professionalization. Furthermore, the premodern form of profession might at some times or for some purposes be preferable to the modern form.

Premodern Meaning

The last comment implies that there has been a considerable shift over the centuries in the meaning of professional. On this point the evidence is clear: in many ways the meaning of professional is the reverse of what it once was. There has also been continuity, of course, but the shedding of the premodern meaning is what interests me here. Is the modern meaning preferable in all ways to the premodern? If some of the premodern meaning is desirable, we may want to retain that which may still exist in the Catholic church.

A simple, dramatic contrast between the premodern and modern understanding of professional can be made with these three points: (1) In the premodern form, the professional lived in the community and served it on a permanent basis. In the modern meaning, there is a "professional community" which supplies individuals to local communities on a temporary basis. (2) In the premodern meaning, a professional was willing to sacrifice money because the work itself was so valuable. The modern professional is the person who expects to get higher pay. (3) In premodern times the professional accepted his or her knowledge as a grace to be shared; the community granted "license" to this person's challenging the community. In its modern form professionals' knowledge and license give them a protected status: the community is not allowed to intrude. Robert Jay Lifton summarizes the shift in this way: It was from advocacy based on faith to possession of technique devoid of advocacy.[5]

The premodern meaning of professional has its roots in the Catholic religious order. A person professed vows, or, more exactly, one was professed in vows. The vowed person stepped before the community to *confess* what he or she was *pro-fessed in.* A lawyer or doctor was supposed to have a comparable dedication to higher values and a loyalty to some chosen community. Obviously, the ideal was often violated, but the ideal was nevertheless clear.

Modern Meaning

The change to a modern meaning of *professional* occurred over a period of centuries during which the very concept of *modern* was born. Individualism, rational science, technology, and international trade helped to bring about the modern world and to define the meaning of modernity. The modernizing of the professional was already advanced in England by the seventeenth century. More professionals existed in increasingly narrow specializations while achieving money and status.

An interesting sidelight is that conditions in the North American colonies delayed the process. The minister, who in the eighteenth century was likely to spend his entire professional life in one local church, might also function as doctor or lawyer. Until 1765 there was no medical school in the colonies. There were few lawyers or, stated differently, nearly everyone functioned as his or her own lawyer. Women, it should be noted, then played a larger role than they would in modern professions which are inherently sex biased.[6] In the nineteenth century, women were allowed into medicine and education as a subprofessional class. They could be nurses and teachers (the paradigm for professional educator was the male administrator), and to this day 95 percent of "professional women" are either teachers or nurses.

When the United States became professionalized in modern form, it did a thorough job. All kinds of groups from engineers to undertakers seized the concept and its modern meaning. In 1850 a leading educator, Jonathan Turner, had pronounced that 5 percent of any population is the professional class; the other 95 percent of society is fit to be the industrial class.[7] The twentieth century seemed to democratize the concept, but there may be a flaw in supposing that the nineteenth century's sex- and class-biased meaning of professional can simply be spread to everyone. When everyone is a professional, who are the clients or consumers? The answer is: all of us. This other side of professionalism, the consumerist culture, is causing increased frustration. A society made up of innumerable niches of expensive and esoteric services is not really what anyone had in mind, but it is what we have increasingly become.[8]

Postmodern Meaning

Thirty years ago no one talked about a crisis in the professions. We may have had too few doctors or engineers, but the solution was clear: more recruitment, higher pay, and better working conditions. What we have today is an attack upon the professions themselves, and the attack is by no means confined to a weird fringe. In one week in 1979 the President of the United States delivered stinging attacks on both the medical and legal professions. Malpractice insurance rates are a symptom of our society's distrust of doctors, the same people who by nearly all criteria constitute the top profession. Some people seem to pine for the premodern world, a sentiment I do not share at all. Anyone familiar with the fourteenth century will not look to it as the golden age of medicine. Nonetheless, we might have to reappropriate some of the premodern meaning of *professional*.

It would be tragic if those of us in church education were fighting today to get into the nineteenth century. Doctors, lawyers, soldiers, engineers, and athletes are experiencing a breakdown in the modern meaning of *professional*. We cannot assume that the meaning is sitting there waiting for our adoption. The world is looking for a "postmodern" meaning of *professional* that may have resemblances to a premodern meaning. The person working at the intersection of church and education is one of the people who could demonstrate a new meaning of professional which is also an old meaning. Every professional in the postmodern era will have to relearn something about religious devotion and on-the-job training. Thus, while a church educator has something to learn from modern professionals, he or she also has something to teach them.

Given the strengths and weaknesses of the Roman Catholic church, an educator there has no choice but to be creative and imaginative. A new meaning of *professional* can and must be created. Central to this meaning is a rethinking of the professional's relation to community (which will allow some different thinking about money). Becoming professional is certainly going to remain highly desirable. In contemporary speech everyone wants to be professional because the opposite of professional is ignorant, unskilled, and incompetent. However, the opposite of our modern professionalist/consumerist culture is not necessarily a culture of ignorance and incompetence. There could be a society in which communities of persons possess a variety of skills with a variety of degrees of training.

The Professions of Church Education

If we grant that church education should be professionalized, what routes exist for it? I think there are two professions that can overlap in church educational work. These two are not simply parallel professions; they reflect different stages of historical development. The first, which I will call *religious educator,* is conceived in the model of a modern profession. The second, which I will call *church minister in education,* has characteristics of a premodern form of profession. My claim is that both professions can and should contribute to a postmodern form of church professionalization.

This position is in contrast to the attempt to make DRE a profession, exemplified by Dorothy Jean Furnish's *DRE/DCE: The History of a Profession.*[9] This book contains some valuable information, but the author's equating of professionalization with the one job of DRE is illogical and self-defeating. The hope at the turn of the century was for a profession of religious education. By 1940 there were less than one thousand people, located exclusively in Protestant churches, who had the title of DRE. In the 1940s nearly all of these people changed their name to Director of Christian Education or Minister of Christian Education. Furnish fails to note the significance of this change—namely, that a profession of religious education had failed to come alive, and therefore these thousand people turned to the existing profession: church ministry.

For many Protestants the last dozen years of Catholic interest in a "profession of DRE" is a case of déjà vu. The Catholics, it is assumed, will soon discover that the profession does not exist and that the institutional obstacles to its creation are overwhelming. Catholics would be well advised to study both the Protestant experience of this century and the contemporary crisis of the professions. If the Catholic church is successfully to professionalize its education, the movement has to be wider than simply putting more DREs in the mold of the modern professional. The Catholic church should learn from its own history and attempt some new alliances in its educational work.

The Two Professions

Anyone working in church education needs the support of some larger group who are engaged in similar work. I will describe the two main forms of professionalization that affect church education:

1) **Religious Education.** The early twentieth century's hope of developing this profession remains largely unfulfilled, but the effort to realize a profession of religious education continues. This profession looks to other parts of education for guidance and support. Credentials are supplied by the university, which certifies a knowledge of education and of religion. The salary expected by a religious educator in a parish would be comparable to that of teachers and administrators in school systems. This salary and the terms of work would be stated in a detailed contract.

2) **Church Ministry in Education.** This whole phrase is seldom used, but it accurately describes the profession of many people in Protestant churches and Catholic parishes. These people look to the profession of ministry (or divinity) for support and for models of action. Credentials, if any, are supplied by a church body; the individual's personal religious life may be considered more important than the degrees he or she has acquired. Instead of a legal contract, there is a formal or informal sign of the community's approbation.

Both professions have drawbacks, but both can be helpful. The problem today is that individuals may not be sure which one they are in. A parish can then get very confused about what it expects from "the professional." For example, most Catholic parishes have no experience in paying their professionals a high salary. A religious educator who asks to be paid a "professional salary" is likely to have a misunderstanding with the parish board over the meaning of that phrase.

The strength of religious education is that it can give the individual freedom of action and adequate recompense. The weakness which I've already admitted is that the profession barely exists. But even were there thousands of well-trained religious educators, would parishes be ready for them and could parishes afford them? The strength of church ministry in education is that it clearly does exist; the local church provides an outlet for the dedication of thousands of people. Some of them have Ph.D.'s, others have not finished elementary school, but that's not the decisive issue here. The weakness of this system is that it can be exploitive of good people, continuing the biases (especially sexual ones) that have been associated with church ministry for centuries.

I should note that the contrast of religious educator and church minister in education overlaps but is not identical with the division of clergy/religious order and laity. This latter contrast is now a source of some conflict in Catholic church education. The conflict cannot be quickly eliminated, but it would help to use the two categories I have described. The fact, for example, that someone is a nun should usually be irrelevant to hiring practices and salary. This suggestion might seem to worsen the financial plight of people called *lay*, but eventually it would be to their benefit. The financial situation of parishes and dioceses would be clearer, and the chances for a more equitable sharing of resources would be increased.

There are people in religious orders who have become professional religious educators. Their larger salaries may corrupt them (or get them into trouble with the IRS), but that's generally not the business of their employer. On the other side, there are people who are called *lay* who are actually church professionals, that is, they are church ministers in education. We ought to acknowledge this fact with a consistent language. For example, the word *lay* does not belong in front of catechist. If someone has received approbation as catechist, then he or she is no longer a lay person in church ministry.

Suggestions for Development

1. RELIGIOUS EDUCATOR

The Christian religious educator needs to develop allies who are not part of the local church/parish. These professional supporters might include religious educators in other parishes, religion teachers in Catholic schools, people in Jewish and other Christian congregations, university and seminary faculties. The religious educator's mission is to bring educational critique to the existing church, including the very existence of parishes. For the sake of a greater church still being born, the religious educator has to work not only with the church but sometimes against the church. This work inevitably includes accusations of heresy or disloyalty. Any religious educator in a parish needs both the temperament for some conflict and the support of professional colleagues beyond the parish.

Religious educator is not a church office. It is a profession free from many of the limitations of ecclesiastical structures. However, the freedom from the limits of the church also means that the profession's financial base cannot rest solely on the church. The religious educator has to realize that his or her full time job prospects in the church are probably restricted to a small group of churches mostly in the suburbs. The other logical possibility is to create a contractual relationship with several rural parishes too small to support this kind of professional, or several urban parishes too poor to afford this service. I know of a few experiments in this alternate form, but we need more data on the possibilities and pitfalls of such organization.

At present only a small number of Catholic parishes can support a professional religious educator; 5 percent would be a reasonable estimate. Many of the rest of us whose identity is religious educator find employment in high schools, seminaries, universities, and consulting firms. I do not think we can complacently settle into this arrangement. A comparison to the legal profession may be helpful here. At the end of Jethro Lieberman's *Crisis at the Bar,*[10] he pinpoints the biggest problem as money. Many lawyers are grossly overpaid, yet most people cannot afford legal services. Lieberman proposes that every lawyer as a requirement to entering the profession devote time working for those who have little money. He admits that his proposal is utopian, but he thinks it should nonetheless be discussed. What he is actually doing is calling the attention of lawyers to a premodern meaning of professional (service to the community) which lawyers still support with their words if not with their cash.

I would suggest that professional religious educators should devote a period of years or a part of each year to people who have little money. For a religious educator in an affluent parish, this could mean a contractual agreement which frees him or her for some hours a week. Such a contribution of time and skill would be a commitment by both the parish and its religious educator to the wider community which is less fortunate. Those of us who draw the high fees of universities and lecture platforms might also contribute some of our time to communities unable to afford a professional religious educator. I don't mean a grudging acceptance of some low paying work, but a public advertising that we are available for some of our working hours to those who can pay us only a nominal sum.

2. CHURCH MINISTER IN EDUCATION

The limitation on church minister in education is almost the opposite of what limits the religious educator. The latter profession hardly exists while the former is part of one of the oldest professions. The role of church minister in education cannot be improved solely by changing the job of the person now in education. The question at issue is the nature of *minister* and *ministry* in the Christian churches.

The professional I am now describing is usually in a local church or parish because that is where most Christian religious communities are to be found. The professional's loyalty is to the community, and the community makes a wide variety of demands. The community may expect the professional to be available at all kinds of hours even though the service required may be simple and unspecialized (supervising a gym, serving meals). The community in turn should support the professional in a variety of ways.

The rewards for this kind of work are not mainly financial. While money is one legitimate sign of support, the church community has a duty to resist the reduction of all values to market terms. The greater reward here is the recognition that one is using God-given talents to help others in educational ways. The main educational effort is to provide people with experiences of belonging to a Christian community. The aim is to develop a community of communities, each with a competence that could be called professional.

Some of the competent and dedicated people who do church work are unpaid volunteers. Others of its professionals are paid but not usually in straight salary. The eighteenth century church provided land to the minister so that he could farm. Today the community may provide housing which, it should be carefully noted, is a symbol of the professional's relation to the community. Other supports (e.g., a car) are less clear symbolically, but they are part of an intricate relation of personal life and professional work. Anyone entering this profession should be aware of the meaning of this financial arrangement. Especially if the person is head of a household, he or she would do well to discuss with his or her family the restrictions built into this profession.

A written agreement can be helpful here, but it does not have to be a legal contract. The need is to avoid misunderstandings by a statement of minimum expectations for professional and community. If there is no trust between these parties, a detailed contract will not substitute for it. Furthermore, a current misconception assumes that the mark of a professional is the contract. Lieberman appeals to an older and richer meaning when he writes: "Professionalism consists in doing right though the sanctions of law are absent."[11] I would like to be protected in my work from exploitation and misunderstandings; nevertheless, I would also like to use my imagination to re-create the job into something neither I nor my hirer can foresee.

A parish isn't to be modeled on the modern university or the nation state. We don't need a bigger professional class to serve more consumers. Minister and ministry should be moving in the direction of encompassing everyone who wishes to devote time, talent, and training to the church. Note that the current interest in many professions to get "paraprofessionals" for the routine work may not be a move in this same direction. We don't need an intermediary class so that the professionals can become more esoteric and protected. A church community should consist of people with a variety of skills (some not credentialed by the university), trained to varying extents. Every parish member should be able to share in the professional work of the church.

The typical Catholic parish, therefore, should have dozens, hundreds, or thousands of "professional ministers." That means a considerable shift in church language and in the allotment of parish resources. A large part of parish money should be used for educating hundreds of the parish's ministers. Would that mean a big cut in pay for the one, two, or three now called ministers? Perhaps. But Catholics in this country have been remarkably generous with money for the church. In many places this generosity is not being tapped today for educational programs that the community can recognize as worthwhile.

The parish should be a reminder to the wider society that its problems can be solved only if people care for each other at the personal, familial, and communal level. If I am able to care, to reconcile, to teach, to counsel, to guide a discussion, I can be part of the church's professional ministry of education. Parishes usually do need someone to coordinate or direct the educational resources of the community; hence a title to that effect can appropriately apply to one of the church's ministers. Parishes can also use the challenge of religious educators who respect current church structure but do not assume it is forever fixed. With the help of people in both professions, the people who are the professing Christians can give witness to the world of a renewed church. This postmodern form of professionalization would draw upon the church's past, accept the history of modern times, and create for the future era communities of teaching and service.

SUMMARY

The main points I have tried to make are:

1) The attempts of Catholics to establish a profession of parish DRE are far too narrowly based.

2) The person directing parish education has a choice between the profession of *church minister* (one of the oldest professions) and the profession of *religious educator* (one still trying to establish itself).

3) *Church minister* shows the marks of the premodern era in its commitment to local community, sacrifice of financial rewards, and possible fluidity in defining membership.

4) *Religious educator* fits the modern concept of professional in its concern for specialized training, wider vision, and adequate pay.

5) The churches can use both kinds of professionals, but pastors, parish councils, and educators need to sort out the several ways of acting professionally.

Parish Models of Education

To apply these points to existing situations, we first have to recognize that the word *parish* does not always refer to the same kind of organization. *Parish* may mean a complex modern organization of thousands of people, or it can mean a few dozen people with a minimum of organization. These two ends of the spectrum have some qualities in common which set them off from the intermediate-sized parish. Just as a large, old city in many ways resembles a rural village more than it resembles its neighboring suburbs, so also the *super parish* and the *mini parish* have much that they share. The intermediate-sized parish is where the greatest confusion lies today, and I will address that question last.

If one is trying to describe the future parish, the place to start is with super parishes. If they are well organized they will have many mini parishes within them. The intermediate-sized parish can learn from both the large and small parishes. Eventually it will have to move in both directions. It must, either on its own or by amalgamation, develop more central organization but at the same time cultivate mini parishes as the basic organizing unit. The policy of simply dividing a parish of 1,500 households into two of 750 may seem logical to a bureaucracy but it makes no sense in communal or educational terms.

1) **The Super Parish.** What can be imagined for a large and well-organized parish? There would be a group or team of ministers who direct the work of the parish in areas of liturgy, social service, and education. The group would be accountable to a council or board elected with the help of the best available political process and means of communication. The inner group of six or eight ministers would divide the work of the parish in a way that fits its specific needs.

One of the people might be called the *minister of education*. The job would be twofold. Internal to the group, he or she would monitor the language, imagery, and direction of the ministerial team to prevent its becoming a bureaucratic élite. Externally, the task would be to involve as many people as possible in the educational ministry of the church. The question is not how to fill eight teaching slots in the church school but how to involve adults and children in hundreds of ways. One person cannot do all that needs doing, but one person can imagine and/or coordinate the efforts. The job might best be done not by a scholar but by someone who has roots in the parish and is already an organizer. The job ought to have a recompense, but the visible support of the parish might be as valuable as money to such a person.

In addition to this core of ministers, a super parish should be able to hire at least one and preferably two *religious educators*. While they may in practice function in close relationship with the parish ministers, they are employed on a different basis and for a different purpose. They bring to the parish a supraparochial vision and the specialized training of the university. Their job is the modern part of education called schooling. Occasionally they would run courses for the parish at large. More often they would teach the teachers of the parish (parents and many other adults). They might engage in their professional work only twelve to eighteen hours a week, but they would be delivering an invaluable resource to the parish.

These modern professionals should be paid the going rate for such professional service. There are many existing parishes that have the money for one, two, or more religious educators, but parishes are still confused about what a religious educator is. Note that the parish school should be an ally rather than a foe in developing the category of "professional religious educator." People know that to maintain a school building and a faculty requires large amounts of money. If a parish is committed to a school, the argument can be made that comparable professional service should be available to the rest of the parish. If a school does not exist or is closing, professional religious educator(s) can be seen as a bargain. In any case, some respected voices in the parish ought to argue for a religious education budget of many tens of thousands of dollars.

2) **The Mini Parish.** The very small parish is likely to be found (a) in rural towns, (b) in depressed urban areas, (c) in experiments of non-geographical communities. In each case the mini parish might learn something from the super parish, and in turn a well-organized super parish should cultivate the mini parish. In the mini parish the organizational question appears to be simple, but key roles still function. There is likely to be only one paid position, and even that one may not be a full-time job. One person cannot do everything, so that his or her main task is to get many people involved in the parish's work. This person, who is probably called the pastor, is also functioning as the minister of educa-

tion. Instead of electing a parish council, it makes more sense for the entire parish to be the board of directors.

One drawback to this informal kind of parish is the lack of a professional religious educator. The mini parish cannot support one. Two ways of adapting are possible: (a) the mini parish might be connected to a super parish that would release one of its religious educators for work with the mini parish. This relation would be especially appropriate where the small parish is urban and poor. The arrangement might free the religious educator for as much as a full day a week or for just an evening a month; the important thing is to start the relationship. (b) The pastor/minister of education might work out a variety of relationships with local colleges, other churches, libraries, businesses, and anyone else who can be of educational help. Many services are free, but people may not know of them. For additional help in religious education, the mini parish might judiciously spend its money for outside consultants.

3) **The Intermediate Parish.** The confusions of church life and especially religious education show up in the medium-sized parish which is not large enough to be an efficient organization and not small enough to be a community inviting everyone's participation. In light of the discusssion of large and small parishes, some clarification might be brought to the confusions of the medium-sized parish.

The person hired to be DRE/coordinator in such a parish is liable to face this situation: (a) be expected to do the two different jobs I have described as church minister of education and religious educator; (b) be paid less than professional educators, but be criticized for being more expensive than other church ministers; (c) be expected to educate the whole parish, but not have either the resources or freedom that education requires. A person who is taking this job should know exactly what crossfire he or she is walking into.

People who become DRE/coordinators in medium-sized parishes are sometimes confused about their own demands. If the person wants everything spelled out in a contract, then he or she cannot logically complain of being treated like an employee rather than a member of the community. The choice isn't always exclusive, but the DRE/coordinator at least has to choose which of the two roles to emphasize. If he or she wishes to be an integral element of the parish ministerial team, then the important thing is building trust and getting an oral understanding with the parish board and other parish ministers. The written agreement becomes brief, secondary, and not really a contract for services.

If by choice or necessity one wishes to be a religious educator in the modern mold, then that fact should be made crystal clear to board, pastor, and everyone else concerned. The limits of the parish demands should be precisely stated, but the other side should also be clear, namely, that the professional religious educator does not expect the parish to be a constant source of community experience and support. The DRE/coordinator here should expect to be treated as neither more nor less than a paid professional. The work can be friendly, enjoyable, and stimulating, but the parish's main sign of support is the paying of a living wage.

Many medium-sized parishes are hiring a DRE/coordinator and working through some inevitable confusion and conflict. The process can represent real progress in the church. However, there are parishes advertising in the press for a DRE/coordinator which should be advised that they don't know what they are doing. Unless a parish can offer a living wage (something above the U.S. government's poverty level for that area) it should probably go another route. This proposal may seem to reduce employment opportunities for educators in search of jobs, but I see little advantage in people getting caught in intolerable situations while being paid scandalously low wages.

I would emphasize that there are alternate routes for a parish to go. If the project is to improve (or professionalize) church education, that is not necessarily accomplished by simply hiring a DRE/coordinator. Should the parish have only $6,000 for this purpose, there are other ways to spend the money than to get one overworked and underpaid person to do the whole job. Why not bring in someone on a temporary basis whose aim would be to organize the existing resources of the parish? For a modest fee a professional religious educator might be found who would be a regular consultant to the parish but not a full time employee. Many university or seminary faculty members would be glad to have the work.

Another worthwhile investment for a parish is educational grants for parish members. Some equitable system has to be devised for distributing the money, but that is not too difficult to do. If a parish is committed to $6,000 worth of religious education, why can't it be in grants of $100 or $300 to the most astute and alive people in the parish? Some of the best students I meet in institutes and graduate programs are there on such diocesan and parish grants. The tragedy is that there are not thousands more of them. At the end of five years the parish could have, not a continuing struggle to hold on to a DRE/coordinator, but a dozen or more of its own professionally trained religious educators.

In summary, the church should not be thinking of trying to professionalize education by hiring one DRE/coordinator for each parish. The two relevant questions are: (1) How do we organize whatever resources already exist in a parish so that most parishioners can be part of the professional ministry of education? (2) How do we bring the critical thinking of the academic world to bear on the parish? The DRE/coordinator can be part of the answer to both questions, but hiring a DRE/coordinator may not be the appropriate response in many situations.

The picture for the very large and very small parishes is clear. For the medium-sized parish, one can only advise: (1) study large and small parishes; (2) take stock of the parish resources and needs; (3) use available money for imaginative and temporary programs in religious education until a larger investment has broad parish support; (4) hire one or more professional religious educators when a good salary can be paid and when parish leaders know exactly what services they need.

8
Can Adult Education Be Religious?

Throughout the first seven chapters of this book my concern has been to define religious education both as a field and as a profession. Considering it as a field, it was necessary to stress that education is not reducible to schooling, despite the great importance of schooling for living in the contemporary world. Education has to include family life, work, and leisure. Based on this model of education, a theory of religious education can thereby include experiences in community, the struggle for social justice, liturgical ritual, and contemplative prayer. Schooling is not exclusively for the young, and the inclusion of nonschooling forms of education seems to be the only way to break the modern identification of school with the child.

As a profession, religious education was described in chapter 7 as closely related to but distinct from the profession of church ministry. The professional religious educator should be centrally concerned with schooling, although not to the exclusion of nonschooling forms. When a religious educator does deal in such forms as "community," the word does not necessarily have an ecclesiastical meaning (for example, the Catholic religious order or the parish). The religious educator's professional commitment has to be to an education that does not exclude any of the ways people are trying to express their religiousness. (The *personal* commitment of the religious educator may have a different emphasis, with the church taking precedence over any educational institution.) How much territory the educator's professional commitment may cover is not clear because we are still trying to discover the varieties of religious expression in the lives of children and adults. Many of the religiously interested are not going to show up for church or synagogue instruction, but anyone who claims the title of religious educator cannot be unmindful of them.

In this chapter and in the three chapters that follow I will try to illustrate that this approach to a field/profession of religious education would help to reconceptualize some long-standing problems. These four chapters are in the nature of case studies in the meaning of religious education. What does religious education have to say about adult education, moral development, the middle-aged man, and education for justice? In each of these four cases I am critical of the church's tendency to take over schemes that are insensitive to or downright antagonistic to a religious outlook.

In the first case, examined in this chapter, I find it depressing to see churches and dioceses importing experts in adult education to solve a religious education problem. The impression one gets from the endless talk about assessment of needs, motivating learners, and packaging programs is that the church has a marketing problem. My suggestion in this chapter goes in a different direction. I claim that the meaning of adult is unclear in the church and even more unclear in the history of adult education. Before the church buys any adult education theory, it should pay heed to its own history and the history of other religions. Some of the techniques of adult education might then prove useful, but only as the meaning of adult education is transformed by a recognition of religious experience and religious language.

At the beginning of a book on catechetical theory which I wrote in the mid-sixties, I suggested that an implication of the theory was the need to shift some educational resources to adults.[1] I was taken by surprise when that one sentence drew more reaction than anything else in the book. At the time I was unaware of how many other people had said similar things both in recent decades and in previous centuries. Since 1965 I have tried to refine the question and say precisely what I favor. Despite the fact that I have never written a book or an article advocating "adult education," I am regularly identified with that camp. Over the past decade and a half I have tried numerous phrases ("adult-centered education," "adult direction," "adult church," "education toward adulthood") as ways of stating the issue, but they have been to little avail. Many people seem to think that the question is a very simple one and that the only problem is money or motivation.

The amazing fact is how long the church has been locked into a fruitless debate in this area and how little progress seems to have been made. I do not mean progress in institutional reform but simply in stating the question. If we go back, for example, to the 1840s we find a battle between two of the giants of the nineteenth century, Orestes Brownson and Horace Bushnell. Their statements could show up in church discussion today without the change of a word, and the speaker might assume it is a new argument:

> We regard the improvement of the adult as the means of advancing the child rather than the education of the child as the means of advancing the adult.[2]

> What a position is given thus to children growing up to look on an

adult church, instructed into the opinion that what they look upon—Christ, ordinances, covenant, vows—is only for adult people.[3]

Both Brownson and Bushnell have hold of some truth here but each also seems oblivious to the ambiguity of his position. Should we not in our day be able to arrive at a better formulation of the question than did these two great men? Brownson argues that if first you can change adults then children will also be changed. That might be true, but we will never know because the children are already being deeply influenced while we are working with the adults. Bushnell contends that if first we can make children be Christian, then we would eventually get a more Christian church. Unfortunately we will never know if that is true because Bushnell presupposes the same unrealistic condition as Brownson's statement. These seemingly opposite positions may therefore be closer together than either would care to admit.

People who argue "educate the child" and their opponents who argue for "adult education" often presuppose the same atomistic and rationalistic world. We would get a different set of choices if we began with the following realities: (1) three or more generations in relationship, (2) the family as a powerful influence, but the family embedded in a matrix of social, political, and economic relations, (3) education as the interplay of learning forms throughout everyone's life, (4) religiousness as ritual, story, and a way of conduct sometimes, but not always, finding expression in the church. If one takes account of these realities, then the formulas of education will not simplistically oppose the child and the adult. Instead, we would be looking for ways to shape and reshape the learning which everyone experiences by getting born into the human community. The more we can encourage the interplay across generations, the richer will be the possibilities of education.

The Adult Education Movement

An adult education movement has existed in this country for at least a century. The roots of the movement could probably be traced back several centuries. Between the world wars there was a giant leap of interest both in theoretical studies and in organized programs.

During the past two decades, adult education has appeared to be on the constant increase. Each fall the Sunday supplements list the nearly unlimited possibilities for adults in search of education in everything from abacus operating to xylophone playing. We are told that, because tens of millions of people are enrolled in programs, adult education has finally come into its own. It even has its niche in the university, where courses called *adult education* are given, and credentials up to the doctorate are conferred.[4]

This proliferation of courses and programs has some obvious advantages. Many people are benefitting from the vast array of offerings that the competitive market sustains. Nonetheless, the very success of adult education, as distinct from the rest of education, raises a question about the theoretical basis of the movement. To this day, when the word *education* is used without a qualifier, it inevitably refers to children. The effect of the word *adult* is to create an exception to what is assumed to be the normal kind of education.

The danger inherent in the phrase *adult education* is that it creates a dichotomy: real education for children and adult (or unreal) education. At an early stage of development, the movement for adult education had to live with this tension and danger. In attempts to change any well established arrangement, reformers are willing to be thought odd. Their defense is usually that the oddness results from their being in touch with an older or a richer tradition which the institution currently neglects because of its particular institutional form. One way that institutions resist reform is by giving the reformers a small place in the established organization.

Adult education, however, no longer functions as a movement within education to change educational institutions. Instead, adult education has successfully arrived at a limited but visible status within certain educational institutions. Many people now wonder whether this achievement is what the whole movement was about. I think the dissatisfaction of some people is reflected in recent moves to change the name of what they are doing. During the past two decades, terms like *continuing education* and *lifelong education* have become prominent.

Continuing education could be a helpful phrase if it were regularly paired with *initial education*.[5] Then education might be conceived of as including specific structures appropriate to young people and other structures, perhaps more diverse and flexible, for the continued education of people throughout their lives. Unfortunately, universities and other powerful institutions do not speak that way. They replace the word *adult* with the word *continuing* and never think to question the nature of the university in the light of this issue. *Continuing education* becomes the name of a set of courses which, while economically attractive to the university, are peripheral to what is considered its main work.

Another common phrase today is *lifelong education*.[6] No one is likely to be opposed to lifelong education, but things that no one opposes are sometimes devoid of concrete meaning. In the hands of its users the phrase *lifelong education* should presumably be a redundancy. After saying that education is lifelong there remains the need to develop distinctions to clarify and reshape educational institutions. Instead of that happening, universities are quick to adopt the nice-sounding phrase *lifelong education.* However illogical it would seem to be, lifelong education often turns out to be the university's adult education courses.

I think that the term *adult education* is not a very helpful one for describing educational aims and programs. Nevertheless, its past and present meaning need to be carefully examined before we propose another name. A new name should indicate a rethinking of what is wrong with the old name. Otherwise, a new name merely hides the problem. The deficiency in the adult education movement was not the use of the word *adult* but in the supposition that that word is unambiguous. Perhaps if the word *adult* were clarified, then the term *adult education* could be useful in describing some aspect of education.

I am especially concerned here with the role that the Christian churches have played and could play in adult education. Churches have the possibility of challenging the limits of educational institutions, but churches badly need historical perspective here. They keep rediscovering adult education as if it had never been heard of before. The church in Boston, as early as the 1640s, was being assigned adult education as its job.[7] The family, the school, the government, and the business world each had their own autonomous spheres of interest. The church's role was largely restricted to one of guiding and persuading individual adults. At regular intervals during the past 340 years, someone has discovered that the future belongs to adult education. The level of rhetoric on this question has been especially high in the last few decades, though it is not clear that the educational practice of churches has significantly changed.

The Meanings of Adult Education

For society as a whole as well as for the Christian churches the question of adult education should be addressed. It is important to note that the question "what is adult education?" includes three different questions. The question can mean: (1) What *could be* the meaning of adult education? (2) What *has been* the meaning of adult education? (3) What *should be* the meaning of adult education?

These three questions when run together generate confusion. They deserve separate answers from diverse sources. The first question of "could be" is a matter of logic and etymology. The second question of "has been" can only be answered with historical facts. The third question of "should be" is a matter for advocacy which goes beyond the first and second answers but has to be keenly aware of them. In our anxiety to insist upon the *real* meaning of adult education (that is, what we think it should be), we may jump too quickly over the first and second questions. The first answer will provide absolute limits and abstract possibilities, the second answer will set out the actual and stubborn limits that advocacy must confront.

1) **What could be the meaning of *adult education?*** Adult education could logically mean one of two things: (a) the education of people who are classified by chronological division as adults. All education that is directed toward grownups or nonchildren would be called *adult education;* (b) the education that has a quality described by the word *adult.* Education with any age group could conceivably be characterized by the word *adult,* though the meaning of this quality needs further spelling out.

Most people would probably assume that the first meaning is what is obviously meant by the term *adult education.* But there is a peculiarity revealed in the fact that in the first case *adult* is a noun and in the second case an adjective. If the first meaning is the only thing intended then why is it not *adults' education?*

To see the problem here it is helpful to compare the word *adult* to *child.* When we see the noun *child* we know the reference is to people who are not yet grownups. When we wish to describe qualities associated with the child we have not only one but two adjectives from which to choose: *childish* and *childlike. Childish* is almost always used in a negative or critical way even when applied to children. A five-year-old may be ordered to "stop being childish." *Childlike* is generally a positive description which can apply to people of any age. In fact, it is more often applied to grownups than to children. A woman might be described as possessing "a beautiful, childlike quality," a statement that in the past was complimentary though today it might sound condescending. If men as well as women are described as childlike that danger is greatly lessened.

The English language, it might be said, is missing two words in that *adult* serves as a noun and two adjectives. Many times *adult* means nothing more than a statement of age. But when someone is said to be not acting in an adult way, there are characteristics and behavior implied in that usage. Ashley Montagu has tried to coin the term *adultish* and in a recent interview warned adults: "don't be adultish."[8] He is obviously playing on a parallel to the word *child* and is implying that there is a constricted way in which grownups try to act their age. His alternative would presumably be *adultlike,* a word that is not used but whose meaning is often implied. In such cases we use *adult* as an adjective to describe growth into full maturity as a human being.

In summary, *adult education* is a combination of words which is ambiguous in meaning. When used as a noun *adult* most often refers to an age group. What is meant by *adult education* might then be clearer if it were called the education of adults. Yet because the word *adult* seems to function as an adjective in the phrase *adult education,* we could interpret *adult* here as primarily not a reference to age but to quality. Adult education would then be a description of education that leads toward an ideal of adulthood.

2) **What has been the meaning of** *adult education?* The answer to this question is determinable by historical facts. As is usually the case, the interpretation of these facts can be disputed. Of the two possible meanings distinguished above, I think that adult education does not fit neatly into one or the other. Adult education from one point of view has been both of those meanings. From another perspective it can be said that it has fulfilled neither of the meanings.

In the claim that adult education has had both meanings I am saying that it has meant (a) the education of people chronologically called *adults,* (b) education of a quality and form designated by the adjective *adult.* In the first case, adult education has been the means of distinguishing sharply between grownups and children. In the second case, the grownups were consciously and unconsciously directed toward living in an adult way. Thus, both meanings have been operative.

I think one can also plausibly argue that adult education has been *neither* the education of adults nor education toward adulthood. In the first case, the movement has never reached more than a minority of adults and even they have usually been reached in a fashion peripheral to their main interests in life. For the past adult education movement to equate itself with the education of adults would be pretentious. Many adults who have received something deserving the name education in their families, their work, and their leisure activities have never participated in what adult education has meant.

In the second case, adult education has failed to offer an adequate meaning of adulthood either in its form of execution or its implied ideals. If I use the distinction above, adult education has been *adultish* rather than *adultlike.* It has mirrored and embodied the limited ideal of adulthood prominent in the culture. Modern systems of schooling have generally sought to outfit the young man with the knowledge and skills to be successful in this world. The adult education movement in its theory has not challenged that assumption but accepted it. Adult education has attempted to give women and disadvantaged men a chance to compete. The good intentions here should not lightly be dismissed. Individual achievements at times have been dramatic, but the unchallenged ideal of *adultish* success has kept adult education in a position of subordination. The men who are called successful have the power to decide how the world will run. Adult education is for everyone else who wants a little share of that power.

3) **What should be the meaning of *adult education?*** If the term *adult education* is salvageable at all, it has to draw upon both the meanings described above. If adult education is to be a useful description of something for the future, it has to respond to this twofold question: (a) How does adult education reach far more adults than it has in the past and reach them in more significant ways? (b) How does adult education advocate and help bring about a much richer meaning of adulthood than the ideal implied in the past? The first point, concerning numbers, will involve organizational and economic changes. The second point, the description of an ideal of genuine adulthood, will require contributions from many sources (e.g., an expanded developmental psychology). However, both points involve a simple paradox that should not be obscured in all the fine detail. The paradox concerns the inclusion of the childlike in the movement toward adulthood.

To the question "how do we reach far more adults than have been reached in the adult education movement," part of the answer is: by not excluding children. And to the question "how do we transcend the rationalistic individualism implicit in adult education history," part of the answer is: by not excluding the childlike. There is no ready language for such education, but we could get our sights in the right direction. We could stop using language which both worsens the division between children and grownups and also obscures the relation of *childlike* and *adultlike.*

The Possibilities of Church Education

For further elaboration of the above distinctions and relations, I turn to the practice of churches. Much of what follows applies to other institutions, but the Christian church is at least one distinctive institution which has a role to play here. Following from the above discussion, the first issue concerns who is educated: the church as an educator of grownups. The second issue concerns the ideal of adulthood: the church as an important contributor to an adequate meaning of being adult.

1) **Church education of adults.** In the church as elsewhere there is certainly a basis for sometimes distinguishing age groups in education.

But the term *adult education* often has the effect of obscuring the question because it seems to say there are only two age groups: children and grownups. When age is crucial, we need much finer distinctions. There are infants, children, youth, young adults, middle adults, and older adults. Further distinctions within these categories may sometimes be needed.

We do need some educational programs in which age is of decisive importance. A forty-year-old has some needs obviously different from those of a seven-year-old. However, the term *adult learner* does little to clarify this issue. At worst it can strengthen existing stereotypes which oppose children and grownups. Some writers seem to think that in the last two decades we have discovered that children and adults learn in sharply contrasting ways. Ironically, this opposition of child and adult is what John Dewey repeatedly criticized under the label of the old education: "We exaggerate the intellectual dependence of childhood so that children are kept in leading strings, and then we exaggerate the independence of adult life from intimacy of contacts and communication with others."[9]

To overcome these stereotypes we need education that brings out the unity of children and adults. Forms which unite the ages ought to be the primary focus for thinking about education, especially in churches. Community experiences and intergenerational groupings ought to be the main settings for a church's educational work. The family is the most obvious group with which to work in this way. However, the individual family itself needs a context of other families and other nonfamilial but personal relationships. A community, that is, a union of humans, needs at least three generations. When such communities exist it becomes obvious that adults and children are not different learning species. If they get the opportunity, a seventy-five-year-old and a five-year-old can teach each other.

What I am advocating here is not difficult to visualize, and it is in fact being done by some churches. Such churches need encouragement because, perhaps without realizing it, they are engaged in a profound struggle. They are challenging much of the foundation on which modern education has been built. The modern assumption has been that to educate requires us to remove a child from the family, place the child in a largely isolated setting (except for children of the same age), and then give the individual child a knowledge for mastering the world. The church school usually accepted this assumption, and the adult study group does not essentially change the picture.

Consider by contrast a day-long program in a parish or local church. The day might proceed in the following pattern: (1) a gathering of the community with some ritual of beginning; (2) groupings by age, interest, or condition: literary discussions for some adults, planning of projects by other adults, child care for infants, games for older children, a film for young people, etc.; (3) lunch time, when family ties are evident but not the exclusive way of grouping; (4) variations on the second segment for the afternoon; (5) a liturgy involving every age group and various interest groups.

A church that ran such a program would be offering an education that is inclusive of adults. The term *adult education* would probably be considered inappropriate to describe such a format. Perhaps in the future adult education may be understood to include intergenerational and communal forms. For the present we could at least stop using bad formulas like the following from a recent essay: "It is clear that adult education, and not that of small children, is the central focus and most important parish commitment."[10] That kind of statement helps neither adults nor children.

2) **Church education for adulthood.** The way in which educational systems operate implies an ideal of adulthood. The opposing of adults and children in most of modern education, including the adult education movement, has assumed and reinforced a narrow meaning of adulthood. Becoming adult has meant leaving behind the qualities of childhood such as spontaneity, playfulness, and mystery. The adultish ideal is to become rational, independent, productive, and secure. When churches uncritically take over the literature and practices of the adult education movement, they adopt a modern secularist ideal of adulthood.

The ideal I am criticizing is unmistakably articulated in a recent book on the philosophy of adult education. Leon McKenzie writes: "Education must help the adult transform himself from a condition of acquiescence to a condition of autonomy. . . . I see as a general and overarching goal of adult education the promotion of the Promethean spirit among adult learners. . . . Promethean existence as a goal for adult education, there-fore, is a penultimate goal; the ultimate goal is the creation of a utopian future."[11] Since the aim is absurdly disproportionate to the means available to adult education, this statement of goal is not likely to have much effect. Nonetheless, I find it shocking that anyone could be writing such state-ments in 1978, apparently oblivious to feminist, ecological, and numerous other criticisms of the Promethean ideal.

The modern ideal of becoming rational and independent is, of course, not a bad thing. It is simply not enough, and ultimately it is not realistic. Life is not rational, nor is any of us independent. The churches ought to bring a religious perspective to challenge the modern ideal. The childlike, I have indicated, is not a rejection of the rational, independent, productive, and secure, but it is a candid recognition of how we humans stand in relation to such qualities.[12] The childlike has a special relation to religiousness throughout history. Christians are familiar with the saying of Jesus that unless you become like a child you cannot enter the kingdom of heaven. Similar sayings can be found in Buddhist, Taoist, and Native American traditions. Each of them says that to become mature is to recover the seriousness of a child at play.

The Christian churches have not always been comfortable in combining the positive meaning of *childlike* with the references in St. Paul to putting away childish things (1 Cor. 13:11). There is a paradox here but not a contradiction. Paul implies the same kind of distinction as existing between the childish as immature (**nēpoi**) and the childlike as offspring and heirs of God (**tekna**). In the fourth chapter of Ephesians he warns against being tossed to and fro like children, while in the fifth chapter he encourages his hearers to be followers of God, as dear children. That is not carelessness or confusion on his part; the paradox of the adult as childlike is at the center of the Christian gospel.[13] The adult education movement in its assumptions, content, and procedures has been oblivious of or antagonistic to this religious paradox.

For over three centuries in this country, society has assigned the task of adult education to the churches. The idea was that the church should encourage individuals to stay in their proper place, or should help the disadvantaged to find a place. The accomplishing of that task was not a bad thing, though it sometimes hid the bigger social changes that were needed. Today the churches might bring forth a different result in this area from what society intended. The churches might demonstrate the significance of intergenerational education. Church is one of the few agencies that cut across both the ages of past history and the ages of the present population.

The church tradition includes material that can challenge the adultish ideal of our rationalistic civilization. It should not be difficult to include the arts, play, and prayer within church education. Such programs can touch people of every age. Out of intergenerational learning there emerges an ideal of adulthood understandable by child and grownup. We move toward an integration of dependence and independence, the rational and the nonrational, life and death.

9
Beyond the Two Stages
of Moral Reasoning

In trying to reach an adequate meaning for the field of religious education, the question of morality or ethics must eventually surface. The relation of morality and religion has been a central concern throughout the history of Western culture. One might get the impression from some literature today that morality, moral development, values, and so forth, were recently discovered, perhaps as an aftermath of Vietnam and Watergate. As with *adult education,* each generation in this country discovers *moral education* as though earlier generations had never heard of it. In reality, the history of the public school in this country is one of unending involvement with moral education. Back through the colonial period we have been a nation almost obsessed by morality and the question of morally forming the young.

One reason for this intense concern with morality is that we have officially excluded religion from our educational institutions, that is, religion in concrete and living forms that might be publicly studied and intelligently grasped. We allow and even encourage a general religious sentiment to pervade political life and the public school but religion that is "divisive" cannot be allowed. The price we pay in reducing religion to sentiment and generalities is that the cohesive possibilities of religious motivation and religious ritual are excluded along with the potentially divisive doctrines. The burden for individual responsibility and social cohesion is turned over to morality or ethics.

A new wave of writing on morality, ethics, and values began in the 1960s and continued throughout the 1970s. This literature has the benefit of twentieth-century studies on child development and can therefore be more specific about when and how children learn whatever morality they learn. I fear, however, that this new body of writing is still afflicted by the old problem, namely, a separation of morality and religion. I think it is possible and desirable to *distinguish* morality and religion. (One distinguishes poles within a unity; one separates two things.) Writers on moral development, ethical teaching, or "values clarification" routinely begin by separating what they are studying from anything that is religion. Having made that premature and total disjunction, they then have either a false world of morality or a world almost devoid of content. All the skilled doctors in the world cannot save the patient if the vital organs are kept in separate rooms.

What these writers are opposed to is either a confusion of ethics and religion or a replacement of ethics by a moralizing religion. The disease is real enough but the cure cannot be achieved by declaration. The attempt at a total dissociation has two bad effects from the beginning: (1) religious concerns keep surreptitiously drifting back into the discussion because people in this country are affected by religion even if they do not wish to be; (2) the positive possibilities of religious attitudes, religious experience, religious ritual, and religious language are not acknowledged and made use of. Writers on morality or ethics often assume a totally un-reconstructed idea of faith/revelation which allows a neat but unreal separation of reason and faith, ethical principles and "revealed precepts." Through many centuries, morality and religion have been integrally related in human hearts and in social groups. A grasp of that intricate relationship requires some instrument of approach other than a cleaver.

In the 1960s Lawrence Kohlberg ridiculed the idea that one could not separate religious content from a scheme of moral development. Kohlberg said his conception was "a complete separation of moral and religious education."[1] Kohlberg's categories dominated the discussion of the 1970s and seemed very attractive to people in religious education. A system that promises a scientific classification of everyone is hard to resist. In recent years Kohlberg has admitted weaknesses in his scheme. The claim to scientific precision has been undercut by empirical evidence that is at least conflicting.[2] Far more important are the assumptions that underlay Kohlberg's original project, assumptions that have not been abandoned in his recent attempts to shore up his system.

One of the steps needed in writing on morality is to reopen the question of the relation between religion and morality. Some of Kohlberg's comments in recent years are an implicit admission that the isolation of moral thinking is not getting at the hard realities of an unjust world.[3] I do not think Kohlberg is inclined to introduce any explicit discussion of religion. So long as religion is excluded on principle, researchers will never get to "moral development" however long they study "moral thinking."

Later in this chapter I refer to Carol Gilligan's criticism of Kohlberg's system.[4] She raises her points through the lens of feminism, but she is also bringing into the discussion religious attitudes and religious lan-guage. She seems no more inclined than Kohlberg to call *religious* the material that she receives in her interviews. But the attitudes of care, compassion, and nonviolence, the language that is marked by double negatives as a way of living in an unjust world, and the sense of responsibil-ity in personal rather than legal terms show profound religious meaning.

She has interviewed women who were considering an abortion, a decision that almost inevitably evokes religious feelings. The Catholic women, of course, see abortion as a religious question, but so do the other women if one understands *religious* in the way I have been using it, rather than assuming that *religious* is equivalent to church rules. So far Gilligan has not developed an alternate system; perhaps that is preferable for now. However much they have avoided religious education in the past, writers on moral education would be considerably helped by the development of an adequate theory of religious education.

In recent decades several important things have been discovered about the child's capacity for moral reasoning, discoveries which go back mainly to one person: Jean Piaget. Every parent and teacher of the young could profit from an acquaintance with Piaget's findings. An unfortunate aspect of the complicated scheme being elaborated today is that people may miss the few certain and important points about the capacity of the child to deal with morality.

I think there has been a grave mistake in trying to turn Piaget's work on children's thinking into a theory of human maturity. Piaget wrote a fascinating book called *The Moral Judgment of the Child.*[5] As the title indicates, the concern is narrowly defined and the results are likewise narrow. Piaget comes up with the limited but solidly based conclusion that children move slowly from a stage of heteronomous to a stage of autonomous moral reasoning. The move from the first to the second stage occurs in the years about six to twelve.

A knowledge of the two stages of moral reasoning that Piaget discovered is helpful for filling out a small slice of life. What lies beyond that segment of age and that power of reasoning can only be filled out by other kinds of study and other languages describing how people actually live. Therein lies the material for theories of development: the relations of adult and adult, adult and child, people and nonhumans. In this chapter I will (1) summarize Piaget's findings from his book of a half-century ago, (2) look at Kohlberg's popular system as a misleading diversion, (3) suggest by means of Gilligan's articles what would be an appropriate way to go beyond Piaget's work.

Jean Piaget will probably go down in history as one of the geniuses of the twentieth century. In what would be a rare example of progress in philosophy he seems to have definitively confirmed Immanuel Kant's contention that the mind constructs its reality. There has been a long-standing dispute over the active or passive nature of the human mind. The debate will probably not disappear, but from now on Piaget's careful plotting of the child's growth in mental constructs has to be included.

Piaget's strength is, of course, his limitation. He has not tried to explain the universe or even to construct a theory of human development. Instead, he has recorded in detail the steps in a child's coming to possess the power of thinking. Piaget started as a biologist and is only interested in knowledge that is biologically useful. Or, put another way, he defines knowledge as biologically useful; what he calls wisdom or value coordination is not within his definition of knowledge.[6]

This knowledge is built up with categories such as space, time, causality, and reciprocity. Children go through a series of steps before they see the world which grownups—having forgotten their childhood—think is the factual or real world. This development is biologically based, so that a seven-year-old trails a ten-year-old in forms of thinking. There are differences determined by age regardless of native ability. On the one side, this means that adults can do little to hasten the arrival of abstract reasoning. On the other side, adults do not have to worry about how to bring children to their full powers of reasoning; adults just have to be concerned with not putting obstacles in the way of what is otherwise inevitable and irreversible growth.

What Piaget revealed is the dark side of children's lives, the experiences that make children aliens in the world of adults. Freud had taught us some of these mysteries, and fairy tales have for centuries been a key to understanding the child's psyche. Piaget added some definite details to the picture. For example, the young child thinks that the moon and sun follow him or her; the child thinks that dreams come in the window at night; the child at first believes that everything which moves is alive.[7]

When we turn to morality, the domain which Piaget studied is defined on the first page of his work: "All morality consists in a system of rules, and the essence of all morality is to be sought for in the respect which the individual acquires for these rules."[8] If morality equals rules, then the study of moral development is clear and easy to chart. It also means that morality must not be extended beyond its limited sphere in human life. The child's capacity to judge about these rules is dependent upon the child's general capacity to abstract and to judge. In Piaget's definition of morality, the child up to five or six is not a moral agent; rules do function in the small child's world but they are not reflected upon as moral rules.

Traditional moral theology had at least part of the truth in talking about an age of reason beginning about age six. However, this age of reason then takes five or six more years to develop. We should have known without Piaget that four-year-olds cannot act immorally, but in the future the point should be clearer than ever. A four-year-old boy cannot put himself in the place of another person. When his mother asks him to stop bothering her because she is busy, it is not moral perversity but intellectual immaturity that leads him to bother her some more.[9]

At the first stage of morality children think of rules as sacred, untouchable, and eternal. They will do so no matter what the adults may attempt. For example, libertarian parents who set up no rules will not prevent children from acquiring rules. Trying to teach a child of seven or eight that one can generalize a rule and allow exceptions on the basis of the situation will probably not work. Piaget complained that adults moved in the opposite direction; that is, he criticized parents and others for reenforcing the already rigid moralism of the child.[10]

The second stage begins parallel with the first and then runs into conflict with it. In this emerging stage, a child begins to see the purpose and the usefulness of rules. The child discovers that rules are not unchangeable and eternal; they are created by humans and can be changed by humans. The intention behind rules is the functioning of a social order. The child begins to grasp the principle of justice understood as an equilibrium of mutual respect. The movement toward this stage is greatly helped by the interplay of children among themselves. Piaget was critical of traditional schooling for reenforcing[11] a regressive egoism that stands in the way of a morality of cooperation.

The last few pages of Piaget's description of the second morality are suggestive of the direction beyond these two stages. After a child can conceive of a crude kind of equalitarian justice, he or she realizes that the social order is not in fact that way. How does one live in an unjust world? How does one act so as to move toward a better human order? Piaget suggests that questions of intimacy, care, compassion, and love now take over.[12] This further development could be called a deepening of the second stage of morality. On the basis of both Piaget's definition of morality and the common understanding of the term, I think it is more appropriate to say that a person moves beyond questions of moral reasoning. For the next seventy or so years the issue of stages of moral reasoning is almost completely irrelevant.

Lawrence Kohlberg has been quoted as saying: "I'd be happy to stop patching up Piaget's assumptions if I could see another boat on the horizon."[13] I would question whether Piaget's assumptions need patching up. I would also question whether what Kohlberg does is to add patches or to overextend and distort the two moralities of Piaget. Like Piaget, Kohlberg has two stages with references to moral rules: (1) an egocentric stage with arbitrary rules externally imposed, (2) a socialized stage with necessary human rules to maintain a social order. Kohlberg adds a further development by positing a way of thinking that is more abstract. Full moral development would be to live by principles of justice disconnected from context and intention.[14] As a description of how some adolescents think, the further stage may be accurate. This stage could also be seen as a description of how our society encourages some men to think of success. But as a stage of progress in moral development, Kohlberg's assumption of a "postconventional" morality is a reenforcing of a dangerous tendency in Western culture.

The words *postconventional stage* imply that living socially is merely a following of conventions. One has developed to the point of accepting these conventions as a necessity of social order. What then joins the conventional and the postconventional? Both are the acceptance of general rules of conduct, but the postconventional is more general and more abstract; almost by definition this is a "higher" morality. The question is whether this is a more desirable basis for human life.

The direction of the postconventional is already signaled by the way Kohlberg makes a distinction within the conventional, that is, between (1) a "good boy/nice girl" orientation, and (2) the "law and order" mentality. To move from doing what pleases others to doing things for the sake of law and order is, in Kohlberg's scheme, moral development. What rather is the case is that something is gained at the expense of something lost. The move to a more impersonal way of moral reasoning can be judged to be progress or not depending on some larger context. That context is not included in Kohlberg because the scheme goes in the direction of more rarified generality.

Only a small percentage of people in the United States supposedly reach this advanced stage of moral reasoning. In other countries where Kohlberg's scheme has been tested, the percentage is much lower.[15] The obvious question is whether the problem is moral underdevelopment in the population studied or else a cultural/class bias in the construction of the system. Most people's thinking does not go in the direction of social contract theory and Kant's categorical imperative. But people may be moving toward the universal by a different route.

Kohlberg's concept of the postconventional does not describe a movement toward the universal. Rather, it is a description of the peculiarly limited way by which the white, Western male has tried to find the universal in the general. That is, abstracting a principle which can be applied everywhere is not to have reached the universal human condition but to have constructed a general rule outside of the human condition.

Kohlberg has often defended himself against the charge that his advanced moral development is individualistic and rationalistic. He claims that the people he ranks highest, Gandhi and King, for example, were in search of a universal community.[16] Indeed they were, but their great contribution was not to talk about an ideal community. Their greatness was in being true to their personal roots and struggling with real, limited communities. Someone can read sophisticated moral reasoning into Martin Luther King Jr., but that is largely irrelevant to his life's work. The strengths and the constraints of black religion are far more important for understanding the man. King lived by a religious faith defined as "an asymmetric reaction to violence." What moved him was not a high-level principle but the oppression of a particular people.

———————

This last point leads me to one of the most provocative and careful criticisms of Kohlberg's theory. Carol Gilligan, who worked with Kohlberg, has put forward a gracious but nonetheless devastating critique.[17] Her articles are written from a feminist perspective, but it might lead one to suspect that similar criticism could be launched on the basis of race, culture, or class. Her intention is to show that we do not yet have a theory of human development because the present relation of the sexes interferes with our obtaining reliable data. She does not idolize the feminist view but claims that men could be helped by taking account of it just as women can be helped by learning from men.

Gilligan's starting point was the finding that women tended to be ranked below men in studies using Kohlberg's scale. Women tended to be classified at the "good boy/nice girl" position; more men than women made it to the "law and order" outlook. Gilligan suspected that instead of being backward, women might be speaking a different language. The great strength of her empirical data is that the women were really deciding something (an abortion of their own pregnancies) in contrast to the somewhat silly dilemmas that Kohlberg asked subjects to comment upon.

Gilligan found two stages of moral development among her subjects: an egocentric, irresponsible stage and a stage of trying to live by society's rules. The expression of the moral reasoning in both stages was determined in part by the expectations that our society has of women. Gilligan also found a stage beyond the two moralities, but it is completely at odds with Kohlberg's conception of the postconventional.

Gilligan identifies an immature stage of development at which the woman's only concern is her survival. Here there is a refusal to accept personal responsibility. At a second stage there is a recognition of the other and an attempt to care for the other.[18] For a woman in our society this can be responsibility with a vengeance; to be good means to sacrifice oneself. Piaget's concept of reciprocity is at work, but it comes out backwards in application. The woman, according to Gilligan, is liable to take responsibility for everyone else while everyone else is to take responsibility for her.

At the "trans-moral" stage the woman reintegrates the concern for her own survival into the responsibility to care for others.[19] One should not do harm to anyone—even to oneself. The conflicts do not disappear, but the question of morality is radically reconstructed. The issue now centers not on individual rights but on care and compassion which are to be inclusive of oneself and the other.

A "principled understanding of nonviolence" is the closest one can come to describing the ideal which emerges beyond the second stage of morality. Nonviolence is not a principle but a way of living; nonviolence is principled in that careful thinking is always a subsidiary element within a life of nonviolence. "To do good to everyone" cannot get beyond the level of generality entangled with mathematical calculations. "To do violence to no one" comes as close as one can to a universal maxim for daily behavior.

When Gilligan posed the Kohlberg dilemmas to women of mature development they often saw the questions as senseless. Instead of uttering principles like "life is more important than property," they said they could not judge. How can you judge behavior without knowing intention and all the particular consequences? Their comments would rank them well down on the Kohlberg scale. Their "failure" follows from an interpersonal bias, that is, compassion, care, and concern for the particular.

One woman who is quoted at length says: "I don't think I use the words *right* and *wrong* anymore. . . . We are talking about an unjust society. . . . If I don't intentionally hurt somebody, that is my contribution to a better society. And so a chunk of that contribution is not to pass judgment on other people, particularly when I don't know the circumstances of why they are doing certain things."[20]

This woman's refusal to judge people is not a case of moral "relativism" but of deeper moral understanding. The woman accepts responsibility for herself to act; however, she acts with the painfully acute awareness that the choice is not between right and wrong but between two evils. A high-level abstraction about the greatest good for the greatest number would at best be an irrelevant view and at worst a dangerous temptation. "All I am sure of," said Tarrou in Camus' *The Plague,* "is that there is the plague and there are the victims. And as far as possible I do not wish to be on the side of the plague."

My hope is not to get people off a Kohlberg wagon and onto a Gilligan wagon. Rather, my intention is to express a strong reservation about one of today's hot items in religious education. It is dismaying to see schemes brought into religious education without a critical eye being cast upon them. Kohlberg's system is at best a stunted description of human development. It is nonreligious or antireligious in its implications and yet it is being celebrated in many textbooks of religious education.

I would have to admit that the assumptions behind Kohlberg's system are not entirely anti-Christian. Modern individualistic rationalism has its roots in an ideological Christianity. Against this strand of Christianity, I would appeal to the Jewish Bible, the New Testament, and the richest strains of familial, communal, sacramental, and contemplative life in church history.

The following three points serve as summary and conclusion:

1) We could all be helped to understand children's human (including moral) development by learning about the sequence of epistemological capacities. To help children's thinking to develop during the years six to twelve, we cannot directly do much. We can provide some raw material, but the forms of thinking emerge on their own. We can try to design helpful environments and can learn when to get out of the way. Children learn from other children, children learn quietly on their own, and children learn from the nonhuman environment. Children who are called "slow learners" are usually just learning something different from what we think they should learn.

This view is not the romantic one that sees the child always unfolding for the best. Some children act viciously and some people's lives become a mess. What do we say of people beyond the age of twelve who seem not to have passed from the first stage of (moral) reasoning to the second? The adult is helped by knowing that it is not from a lack of reasoning power that the person stays mired in egocentricity. Something has obstructed the exercise of a power whose arrival is biologically determined. The adult may have to devise some compensatory structure to help children and other adults get the functioning of moral reasoning unblocked.

This problem seems to be the basis of Kohlberg's recent work with what he calls the "Just Community."[21] Piaget discovered that children learn about social order by playing games of marbles. If something comparable to marbles is not available in people's lives, then we may have to devise experiences of cooperation, participation, and democracy. Such experiences of community could be provided by the church, the school, the Boy Scouts, the Little League, and dozens of other organizations. Kohlberg's Just Community, a group working out their problems cooperatively, is a modest step but a step in the right direction. In contrast, Kohlberg's recent conversion to "indoctrination" is an unfortunate and defensive move to shore up a collapsing structure.[22]

2) We urgently need a theory of human and religious development, but we are nowhere near having one. Erikson's outline of the "Eight Ages of Man" is still probably the best one available.[23] In a way, however, Erikson is already too detailed and too definite. Eight stages are a more complex

arrangement than either Erikson or anyone else can at present substantiate. In addition, despite his attempt to work a cyclical and synthesizing movement into the stages, their description (and the graph Erikson uses) comes out looking like a straight line of development.

A key to reformulating "the eight ages of man" is the feminist perspective. Erikson has been criticized by feminist writers despite the fact that he was aware of possible sexual bias. He does distinguish between boys and girls, but I think his eight ages are not capable of assimilating the different data. Erikson should not be attacked because he lacks an adequate framework; everyone else has the same problem. The best one can do today is to create an inner dialectic in any scheme of development. The categories should be amenable to an interplay reflective in part of the unresolved questions of sexual relationships.

As a way of simplifying but strengthening Erikson's stages, they could be reformulated this way: (1) trust; (2) autonomy-initiative-industry-identity; (3) intimacy/generativity; (4) integrity. The four words in number 2 are possible short steps within a single move toward the separate individual. In number 3 the two words are an inseparable relation which describes the grownup's involvement, participated in differently by men and women. And number 4 is simply the name of what is being synthesized in numbers 1, 2, and 3.

This simplicity would heighten the significance of religion in life. Erikson comments at length on religion's place in the first age and more briefly on its place in the last age. Religion also belongs in adolescence; indeed adolescence was first defined as the time of religious conversion. What really needs study today is the relation of religion to the adult involvements of love and work. Neither Erikson nor contemporary writers on "midlife" have much to say about religion mainly because their notions of religion are limited to childish dependence or else belief systems.[24] We lack instruments or the eyes to see the religion embodied in work and in love.

3) The step beyond morality indicated by Piaget and filled out in part by Gilligan should be recognizable to religious people. The religious traditions have plenty of material for the understanding of adult behavior. An adolescent is someone still looking for a way to live by uncompromised principles and still attracted by a moral perch above the messy human situation. The person of adult religiousness is sure of one thing: that the adolescent answer is the wrong one.

The main religious traditions are remarkably unified in (1) seeing the need for compassion, love, and care; (2) seeing that however good the world should be or could be, our actual decisions are entangled in evil or sin. Each religious body in its own way warns us that we cannot save ourselves but that, as part of something greater, we will stop asking: How do I do the right thing to save myself? Religions teach a discipline so that we will be able to resist evil. This stance produces a peculiarly negative sounding language. If you look closely you find it is a language of double negatives and thus a language of affirmation in the real world.

Someone is always trying to rewrite the Ten Commandments into positive injunctions. Such people do not understand that "do not kill" and "do not steal" are affirmations; the double negative frees the individual to trust life. When the first epistle of John says that it is by confessing our sins that we are saved, it affirms God's power by the recognition of our own failures. When St. Paul warns us in Romans not to judge others, he is following the example given by Jesus in John's Gospel. The refusal to judge others is not a denial of morality but the attainment of a more inclusive understanding than morality offers.

It is time for religious education to stop being concerned so much with moral stages. Most people have moved from number 1 to number 2 by adolescence. It is time to recognize the richness of our religious tradition to provide for what follows the second stage of moral reasoning. Even for people whose moral growth seems arrested at selfish egocentrism, involvement in practices of charity or prayer is probably more helpful than trying to get at their moral reasoning.

For people who have reached an adult stage of religiousness the illusion of constructing a world according to egalitarian principles of justice has been stripped away. Nonetheless, such people are passionate in their opposing oppression and their serving the needs of others. Very likely there are tens of millions of people in this country who have reached this advanced stage of development; they go through each day with care, compassion, and an active desire to reduce the sufferings of this world. Religious education should dissociate itself from the snobbish arrogance of the moral development scheme and start attending to the saints in our midst. In the following chapter, I comment in some detail on one part of the adult population: men at midlife.

10
Religious Education
for Middle-Aged Men

The decade of the 1970s saw the emergence of a new body of literature concerned with adult development. The event which brought this concern to popular attention was the publication of Gail Sheehy's book *Passages* in 1976. The extraordinary sales of that book revealed a large audience eager to hear about the changes which adults go through in the course of their lives. As one might have expected, many other books and articles followed upon the publication of *Passages*. Neither Sheehy nor anyone else has been able to resolve the methodological problems in this area, three of which might be noted here.

1) It takes longer than any one person's lifetime to gather comprehensive data on development throughout a lifespan. This problem is a large one, but it is possible to cope with it because scientific cooperation goes on across the generations. Researchers today are benefiting from studies begun in California in the 1920s and a study started at Harvard in the 1940s.[1] The problem of getting the data, therefore, is in principle soluble, but we have to remember how sketchy and questionable any present study is.

2) The second problem is in part a result of the first: the data that have been collected are distorted by bias, and the bias cannot quickly be corrected. Studies that were begun several decades ago were not as careful about sexual, racial, national, and other kinds of bias as research would be today. The sexual bias, which is one of the most severe, is also one of the most important. A strength of Sheehy's book is her attempt to take account of the sexual bias in most of the previous studies. Where Sheehy is not helpful is in recognizing a religious bias that affects studies of adult development. If one studies Harvard students of the 1940s, religion may seem of minor importance. If one were to cross the Charles River and study the men and women of an ethnic neighborhood in Boston, religion might appear to be very important. Furthermore, while people today are trying to correct the sexual and racial bias, the same advance cannot be presumed for religion. Researchers still tend to identify religion with "beliefs" or church attendance, neither of which is assumed to be central to

human maturity. We still lack adequate categories and instruments to investigate the attitudes, experiences, rituals, symbols, language, and behavior that deserve the name *religious.*

3) The assumption that there are stages of development in adult lives similar to stages of child development is tantalizingly attractive but probably fallacious. A child goes through some obvious stages of biological growth. The child also goes through a series of steps in reaching the stage of abstract thinking. (In recent times this development has been called *cognitive,* a word that hides the fact that this topic is only one kind of knowledge.) Any attempt to fit adult lives into three, four, or eight age categories confronts the bewildering social complexity of adult lives. I would not deny the possibility of discovering some patterns. It is obvious now, if it had not been before, that adults mature, develop, and go through life shifts. However a universal scheme of ages and stages is probably the wrong thing to be expecting.

Despite the difficulty of describing overall patterns, a few junctures in life have attracted much research. Several monographs of the past decade have described what is called "the midlife crisis." One could speculate that all the talk about midlife crisis may be the inspiration if not the cause of many crises. Still, there is enough evidence to suggest that most if not all men undergo a profound shaking up somewhere toward the middle of their lives.

One of the limited but controlled studies of men in their forties is Daniel Levinson's *Seasons of a Man's Life.* The author found that for 80 percent of the men in his study:

> Their Mid-Life Transition is a time of moderate or severe crisis. Every aspect of their lives comes into question, and they are horrified by much that is revealed. They are full of recriminations against themselves and others. They cannot go on as before but need time to choose a new path or modify the old one.[2]

Note that as part of his description Levinson uses the words *horrified* and *recriminations.* A broader study which places the middle-aged man in context finds these negative elements heightened. Throughout Marjorie Lowenthal's *Four Stages of Life,* the middle-aged man in comparison to younger or older men and in comparison to women comes out looking bleak. "They took by far the grimmest view of the next five years. . . . They seemed to be mustering all their strength to get themselves through another ten or fifteen years on the job."[3]

This male crisis deserves the name *spiritual* or *religious,* but our culture cannot quite admit this fact. One of Carl Jung's best-known statements is his judgment that everyone over thirty-five years old who came to see him had a religious problem. Jung says almost jokingly that perhaps we need schools for the middle-aged. He then adds that churches are supposed to perform this function. On this point I think that Jung is right. The churches may be missing *the* great religious moment in a man's life, at least before the moment of dying.

I am not aware that churches have done much to direct religious education to the experience of the middle-aged man. The church's education has traditionally been directed to children. Adolescence was first defined in the nineteenth century as the moment of conversion; church educational programs after adolescence would be superfluous. Where adult education has been offered it has been mainly for women. The problem here is not just the neglect of a segment of the population. The absence of adult males is a sign that the very meaning of religious education is deficient.

I am proposing here that any activity called *religious education* needs testing out in relation to middle-aged men. That is not to say they are more important than other groups, but rather that they illustrate well the problems and possibilities of a field of religious education. Our culture is willing to grant that religion is for children and old people; there is also a long tradition that assigns religion to women. What has not been readily acceptable is religion for middle-aged men. The issue is not merely one of including men under this category but of rethinking the category of religion when the problems of middle-aged males are named *religious.*

The above paragraph indicates my reason for choosing to focus on men. No one can say for certain what are the significant differences here between men and women. In describing the problems of men and the help that men need, I am not denying anything concerning women. I am simply implying that someone more qualified than I am should write about religious education for middle-aged women. As a general principle, religious education should be a lifelong process with special attention to moments of crisis. The scant evidence so far indicates considerable differences between men and women concerning the timing and quality of life's crises.

The male midlife crisis centers about a single theme, namely, mortality. I will look briefly at the sense of mortality and the reasons for its appearance at midlife. In response to the recognition that all things human die, a man has two major needs: (1) an attitude of irony, (2) a ritual for mourning. After describing what is involved in each of these activities I will suggest a few ways that churches and other religious organizations might be of help. Religious education should be one of the sources for meeting these two needs, while they in turn may help us to think through an adequate meaning of religious education.

It is a peculiar fact that men discover they are mortal only at about the age of forty. Of course, they don't discover the fact of death at that time, but at an earlier age they may have successfully hidden their own vulnerability. Everything in the life of a little boy conspires to convince him that he should grow up to be strong, successful, and unafraid. The ideal has changed little from James Fenimore Cooper's *Deerslayer* to Michael Cimino's *Deer Hunter.* The movie's hero is described as a "control freak": cool, calculating, and fearless. He knows that determined strength can overcome any force of evil.

Sometimes it is the first heart attack that teaches a man differently. (Men between thirty-five and forty-five have three times as many heart attacks as women do—though women will soon be closing the gap.) Sometimes it is less obvious warning signs that bring on a change of attitude. Then the claim of the self-help manuals (e.g., *Your Erroneous Zones*) that you can do anything you wish is exposed as patently false.

The middle-aged man discovers that humans are finite. The word *finite* is a synonym for limit. At middle age the feeling of limitation is suddenly on all sides. Early in life a limit is something to be transcended; the man is always pushing beyond it. Late in life limits can be very comfortable; they allow a quiet space for rest. At midlife limits are confusing but, good or bad, they are undeniable.

First, there is the limit of his job. For a man the job has been the dominant factor in defining success. The standard question among men traveling on airplanes—"who are you with"—is never interpreted to refer to wife or friends. Work is assumed to be the contribution that a man makes to eternity. But somewhere in the middle of life it becomes apparent that the job will not make him immortal. Even if a man has been called successful the idea of limits pops into view. Indeed, successful men feel the problem even more than the unsuccessful; the latter can still cherish hopes of getting to the top. But the problem eventually hits both rich and poor. It is exacerbated by our economy and the insubstantial quality of most work. The haunting spectre for factory men, says Studs Terkel in *Working*, is "the phased obsolescence of people that is a piece with the planned obsolescence of the things they make."[4]

Second, the middle-aged man is likely to be facing problems with his parents. If the parents are aged and ill they are a heavy responsibility. Even with money and good will he may not know what to do. If the parents, especially the father, are strong and assertive they can still dominate the life of the middle-aged man. George Vaillant's *Adaptation to Life* is most remarkable in showing the powerful influence which fathers still exercise in the lives of successful forty-year-olds. If the parents have recently died or are near death they are a reminder to the son that he is next. According to Margaret Mead, we are the first generation in the West that frequently has both parents alive when we have grown to middle age. Logically, perhaps, this fortunate situation should make us grateful and lessen the impact of our parents' deaths. In fact, their deaths may confuse us the more when we have grown to adulthood always assuming their presence.

Third, the middle-aged man is often shifting precariously in relation to his wife. Fiction and real life are filled with examples of forty-year-old men who bolt from apparently happy marriages of many years. The man is often looking for reassurance from one woman or another. If his wife tries to comfort the man in his anxieties, he is liable to feel smothered by mothering. If, as is frequently the case today, she is starting her own new career, the man may feel confused and alone. She starts seeing bright new visions of the work world while he starts looking for compassion and companionship to get through what has become a tedious job.

Finally, there is the limit revealed in relation to his growing children. They are usually at an age which does not offer emotional solace to the parent. The vitality of adolescence and youth makes a man aware that his own youth has passed. He is likely to feel envy toward young men and to feel guilty about the feeling. He is likely to be attracted by young women and have no way to deal with those feelings. Even if a man does not have children of his own, he still experiences the same mixed feelings about young people.

At this moment the man may need a number of helps. He might be able to use some counseling to help his relations to spouse and children. He may need retraining in his old job or may even need an entirely new career. He probably could use a doctor's appointment to get reassurance that half the people his age have a mysterious pain in the upper arm. Also, he may need new forms of leisure that will help him to develop a more interior life. All of these steps are quite realistic and could make a dramatic change in his life.

With these changes, however, a man does need something more. His discovery of mortality—signaled in each of the limit situations above—is a genuine and valuable insight. The proper response is not to cover it with palliatives but to face up to the need for a basic change in philosophic outlook. The attitude which can best deal with death is irony. In addition to that attitude, a man needs a ritual for mourning. With these two pos- sessions he can bring to a conclusion the journey of the first half of life and take up a new search. As Levinson notes, the search for immortality doesn't cease at midlife, it becomes "more conscious, more subject to reflective thought, more modest and realistic in its aims."[5]

Irony is the attitude I wish to describe, an attitude which finds expres- sion in paradoxical forms of speech. I realize that the word *ironic* is used today in a broader sense to refer to anything strangely unexpected. Also, the word *irony* connotes to some people the sarcastic or cynical. But here I am trying to recover the root meaning of *irony* as a philosophic outlook on the human condition.

Irony with respect to the human condition is the capacity to hold simultaneously two seemingly contradictory views of the human being: greatest thing in creation/absurdly small and fragile creature. This attitude has become indispensable in the twentieth century. The successes of Western science and technology have put humans in control of things to an astounding degree. That very success enables humans to see how small and fragile they are in a universe of unimaginable size and energy. Humans are the most important inhabitants of the universe, but at the same time they keep dying at every moment.

Although irony is necessary for living in today's world, this fact becomes evident to a man only when he comes to midlife. A recent book complains that "there is something awry 'in the nature of things' if irony is the highest form of consciousness. Children are not ironical."[6] The writer is correct in saying that children neither have nor need irony, but why assume that children have the "highest form of consciousness"? Although I praised the childlike in chapter 8, I did not equate it with the "adultlike"; one of the missing ingredients in the childlike is irony. If growing up and maturing mean something, they involve acquiring a simple outlook with a complex structure.

Three characteristics help to define irony, and the three can be both cause and effect in its development. Although children are not ironic, the soil of irony can be cultivated from childhood. Then in midlife these three qualities can blossom in their effect while the experiences of midlife can add to their further growth. The three characteristics which I will describe are: (1) a sense of tradition, (2) a sense of centeredness, (3) a special sense of humor.

A sense of tradition means loving one's people and being loyal to them. The young boy thinks that his people are the only reality or the best reality. He judges others as strange or inferior because they do not conform to the codes he assumes are normal. A middle-aged man knows that "my people" are merely a group of people. He comes to see the real and sometimes shocking limitations of his own people. Tradition means a willingness to accept "my people," limitations and all. For the man who has dreamed dreams and seen visions, his own people are a tiny part of the picture, but he loves them more than he could have when he assumed they were the whole picture.

Irony extends this sense of tradition further. For each human being "my people" is the human itself. A modern secularist philosophy that presumes to call itself "humanism" often sounds as if the human were all there is. That position appears ridiculous as soon as one considers the human dependence on soil, oceans, sun, air, and so forth. Humans are neither more nor less than a tiny part of the picture. Solemn pronouncements of modern philosophy could occasionally use some biting wit. The human capacity for pompousness needs puncturing with irony.

The proudest possession of humans is consciousness. Irony is a sharpening of consciousness to a razor-like edge. To be complete, irony has to turn the instrument on the instrument itself so that we laugh at even our proudest possession. "Consciousness ought to play first violin but not be conductor," writes Martin Buber.[7] How do we keep it there in its front seat? By ironically poking fun at its self-importance. No modern writer has honed the edge of irony sharper than has Samuel Beckett. In *Endgame* one character says: "You can reason to your heart's content but the fog won't lift." Another character in *Malone Dies* goes further: "The loss of consciousness was for me never a great loss." The characters in Beckett stubbornly resist unconsciousness, but they are painfully aware that consciousness reveals the ultimate powerlessness of the human to save itself.

The second characteristic of irony is a search for the center. Centeredness is demanded by consciousness, and modern times with its heightened consciousness is also marked by a stronger search for the center of things. One of the most widespread falsehoods is the statement that the Copernican revolution removed humans from the center of the world. On the contrary, modern science and philosophy for the first time and irreversibly placed human consciousness at the center of everything. Kant and Piaget completed what Galileo and Copernicus began. There is no experience which is not human experience; there are no words except human words. All attempts to dwarf the human as meaningless can only be rendered in human meanings.

Irony recognizes that human consciousness is centered in a body located on the earth. The immense power of thinking is absurdly connected to a fragile organism that is dependent on a tiny sphere called *earth.* Every people lives in a place; the more they live there, the more it is a place, their place. Humans also have their place, which is the earth. It is their only place even though its limits make them dream of the far-away stars. "You are on earth and there is no cure for that." (*Endgame*). According to Mircea Eliade, the search of "religious man" is for the navel of the universe, the exact center where everything is at peace.[8] "I have spent my life looking for the center," says Beckett's *Unnamable,* "and nothing is less certain than that I have found it." The one certainty of the clowns in *Waiting for Godot* is that they will refuse to leave the center of the stage which is earth until they get some sign that they were really there.

The third characteristic of irony is a special sense of humor that is based on paradox. The humor here does not consist of jokes about funny topics. It comes out as serious statements that are undercut by some obvious fact about the human condition. The laughter may be an embarrassed kind because the person speaking seems to be deadly serious. The adjective *deadly* is precisely the issue. Mortality is experienced as a bad joke made possible by the location of consciousness in a fragile body.

The solemn and humorless people who think they are getting things under control have no sense of the world's dimensions. Irony is a form of humor which merely recognizes our actual situation. Human efforts at control are paltry, as when Woody Allen notes: "Astronomers talk of an inhabited planet named Quelm, so distant from earth that a man traveling at the speed of light would take 6 million years to get there, although they are planning a new express route that will cut 2 hours off the trip."[9] Humans have unlimited desires and elaborate plans, but they have an extremely limited life span. "They give birth astride of a grave, the light gleams an instant, then it's night once more." (*Waiting for Godot*). The solemnly serious people who want everyone to work hard to improve things don't know how bad things really are: someone out there is killing us. The comically serious (i.e., ironic) people know that only humor can cope with death by putting it at the center of life. "The human condition may be desperate but it is not unequivocally serious."[10]

I would note here that our Western religious traditions abound in irony though we often lack the capacity to recognize it. The sayings of Jesus, and especially his parables, are finely honed irony. The reaction to the Beatitudes was almost certainly embarrassed laughter. Jesus took an established literary form and filled it with a content that approaches absurdity.

The parables are the finest examples of ironic humor. They start from the most commonplace experiences, but each has a sudden little twist that pulls the rug out from under our feet. For long periods in Christian history the parables were misunderstood as moralistic tales, that is, as stories from which one draws a moral application. A moral change is not excluded, but the parables are after bigger things. The parables cut deeply into human pretentiousness and challenge our assumptions about the universe. Human attempts to make the world right usually assume a principle of fairness and equality. What then does one do with the Prodigal Son, the Good Samaritan, and the Laborers in the Vineyard? The parables remind us that though we may be smart we are not all-knowing, that God's way of looking at things may be different from ours, and that unless we can laugh at ourselves we are sure to overestimate our grasp of things.[11]

One reason we do not see the ironic humor of the New Testament is that Christianity removed it from its Jewish context. As indicated above, irony requires a tradition, a sense of the people. The Jews remain unsurpassed in the development of this aspect of irony. The Jewish claim to be God's chosen people has never been more ironic and more relevant than it is today. *Chosen people* is a Jewish joke that makes suffering bearable. The Jews don't claim to be a superior people; they just claim to be superior because they are people. They see themselves as stand-ins for the real chosen people, namely, humans. Jewish history is a reminder that the claim to superiority can only be made from the fragile center of things, not from the top. Human superiority lies not in the power to control but in the ability to receive.

The Christian religion ought to view Jesus, not at the top or the end, but at the center. The Christian mission can be carried out only within the context of Judaism and in relation to other religions that search for the center. Every middle-aged man has to find out the fact which Jesus of Nazareth apparently discovered a few years prematurely: life at the center of things includes the acceptance of death.

Dying is not what one does in the last moment, nor is it a terror from which one should flee. Death is a constant companion playfully kept at bay so long as we are given another day to live. Resurrection is the Christian formula for denying that death is annihilation. A positive sense of resurrection awaits our discovery of the joys and sorrows of life. Death/resurrection is a story that can be known in childhood as a fact. Death/resurrection is a reality that can begin to be lived daily in the experience of the middle-aged man.

Mourning is a simpler phenomenon than irony, but just as important. The need to mourn is a natural consequence of the sense of mortality. Mourning is a nonverbal complement to ironic forms of speech. The ironic outlook is at the edge of despair and is always in danger of turning bitter. Facility with words allows a detachment from the sense of desperation, and thus we are not engulfed by our feelings. But detachment is only one moment in our living with a people, in a place, and under the sign of death. Mourning is the necessary admission that we are not disconnected from the simplest human feelings: sadness, guilt, terror, and reconciliation.

The middle-aged man "reworks his life experiences and his feelings until he is all mourned out and no longer afraid of being mortal."[12] He has to mourn for his parents who have recently died or are entering the last part of life. He has to mourn for his youth, so highly prized in our culture, but forever gone. He has to mourn for his work, which is no longer exciting and is now so obviously transient in its effect. He has to mourn the breakup of personal friendships, which may have come down to a precious few.

Geoffrey Gorer, in his detailed study of mourning, maintains: "At present death and mourning are treated with much the same prudery as sexual impulses were a century ago."[13] This situation is especially hard on the middle-aged man. If he cannot mourn, his life will appear as a steep decline, and he will be gripped by melancholia or fits of irrational anger. Thomas Wolfe in *Look Homeward Angel,* describes Gant: "He was fifty, he had a tragic consciousness of time—he saw the passionate fullness of his life on the wane and he cast about him like a senseless and infuriated beast." If a man cannot mourn for his parents, he is liable to jump a generation and begin imitating his parents, old before his time. If he cannot mourn for his youth, he is liable to be resentful of young people, including his own children.

The difficulty with mourning is that it requires some kind of ritual, a fact that most literature on mourning neglects.[14] The individual man cannot solve this problem because ritual is symbolic and social. From before he can remember, a boy in our culture is socialized away from mourning. "Big boys don't cry." To be strong in bereavement is equated with acting so that no one could guess what has happened. By middle age most men are almost physically incapable of weeping. Even if a man can cry, there is no place in public where mourning men are allowed.

Some recent forms of therapy try to surmount the problem of suppression or repression by unleashing torrents of emotion. Perhaps as a first step in some treatments a direct attack on rage and sorrow will help. Unfortunately, such a tactic may only further deny the need and the value of ritual. Mourning requires a ritual for three reasons: (1) it satisfies the need of the mourner for both companionship and privacy; (2) it allows expression of grief without embarrassment or reticence; (3) it provides for weeks or months of rehabilitation similar to the period after physical illness.

Churches cannot cure this problem in our culture, but they might ameliorate it through liturgical forms and educational practices. The most obvious liturgical form for mourning is the funeral rite. It is probably the most universal and the oldest religious ritual in human history. Each group surrounds the death and burial of a member of the community with a careful ceremony that allows for the expression of sorrow, hope, and common support.

The Catholic church, for example, retains a structured and somber ritual for wake, funeral mass, and burial. There may be a tendency in the post-Vatican II era to drop the *Dies Irae* mentality. Joy and resurrection are the theme of burial ceremonies today rather than dread and guilt; nearly everyone welcomes the change. Still, a caution has to be expressed. Belief in resurrection is not a denial of loss by death. Resurrection belongs at the center of a ritual of mourning for the dead. Those who feel the loss deeply must have a place to express sorrow and be allowed their passage of time for mourning. The funeral mass followed by remembrances at a month, six months, and a year recognizes the natural cycle of sorrow. "In mourning," wrote Proust, "it is necessary to inform every cell of the body of what has been lost."

A more frequent liturgical form is needed to reconcile oneself with ordinary failures, sorrows, and conflicts in life. The Catholic sacrament which used to be called Penance or Confession did have some of that meaning when it functioned well. The attempted reform of this sacrament has simply left it inoperative in the lives of most Catholics. Perhaps some day the reform will be completed, and a sacrament of reconciliation will really be celebrated. The Catholic religious order developed elaborate rituals of confession, penance, and reconciliation, none of which seemed to have worked very well in modern times. The Catholic church's task for the present is to keep alive some ritualizing of sorrow within the Eucharistic liturgy. In addition it has to continue efforts to find appropriate form for a communally celebrated sacrament of reconciliation. We also need some ecumenical study of the forms which confession of sin has taken in Protestant, Jewish, Muslim, and other religious groups.

Besides being aided by liturgical participation, the middle-aged man's religious education might be furthered by his becoming a teacher or counselor. Men who have spent their adult lives teaching young people will find nothing novel in this suggestion. But few middle-aged men have had the opportunity to remain in contact with youth. A man's own children may give him immediate contact, but at the moment of midlife crisis when he needs a nurturing exchange with youth, his own children are probably looking for freedom. Many of those men who have been teachers or counselors for twenty years could use a change of work, at least temporarily. Men who have been working in offices and factories could be helped by becoming teachers.

A civil engineer or a business executive is not likely to become a full-time teacher in a high school. But he could easily become a part-time teacher in the church or synagogue. Few middle-aged men will answer the call to teach a CCD or Sunday School class. They need an invitation to share their feelings about life and work in an appropriate setting, perhaps in a home or where they work. Many middle-aged men would be flattered if someone invited them to talk about what interests them and saddens them. Youth for their part urgently need to hear middle-aged men talk about life with simple feelings and chastened hopes.

This approach would broaden the pool of volunteer teachers beyond the women who now carry the burden. But the proposal is also meant to serve the men who volunteer. Teaching and counseling provide rituals for the expression of sorrow, confusion, hope, and reconciliation. Erik Erikson, who developed the notion of generativity as the task of middle adulthood, has stressed in recent years the real danger of failing at this task. "Adult man is so constituted as to *need to be needed* lest he suffer the mental deformation of self-absorption, in which he becomes his own infant and pet."[15]

A young man in our culture seems to need a "mentor," someone whom he can look to for example and guidance. This relationship temporarily stabilizes his life, but there is a flaw in the idea of mentor. The mentor relation is a paternalistic one against which every healthy adult must rebel. The breakup of the mentor relationship is often tinged with anger and resentment. What the young adult man now needs is not the figure of a father but the reality of a brother. He needs some friends among the men, women, children, and nonhumans on the earth. The absence of friends in the lives of adult men is a rather well kept secret. In summarizing his study, Levinson writes: "As a tentative generalization we would say that close friendship with a man or woman is rarely experienced by American men."[16]

In teaching, counseling, coaching, or any other significant activity of church and synagogue, the middle-aged man should be able to find some fraternal support. Whatever helps to situate him with a sense of tradition and a sense of place is religiously educational. Whatever provides a ritual expression for the tragic feelings of life lost is also part of religious education. With that resituated stability and with reconciliation to death as well as life he is ready to begin part two of his journey.

11
Religious Education
for Justice

In this concluding chapter I return to the theme I began with: the urgent and practical necessity of religious education. Nowhere is the need for religious education more evident than in the struggle for social justice. Individuals, groups, and nations cry out for justice today. How can anyone make sense of what is often a cacophony of claims and counter-claims? There are other approaches to the question of social justice, but in any long view of the matter it is both an educational and a religious question.

As the last chapter tested out the meaning of religious education in relation to middle-aged men, so in this chapter the search for social justice will indicate the adequacy of this book's model of religious education. I have described religious education as inclusive of schooling in religion but also including community, work, and contemplative wisdom. Two considerations guide my reflection on the relation of religious education and justice: (1) How does one define religious education so that issues of justice are the center of the process itself rather than optional content? (2) How do we attend to the entire range of justice issues rather than seeing only the obvious and faddish ones?

My response to these two questions is to propose a process of religious education that always moves in the direction of justice. As the previous chapters may suggest, the movement is slow and calm, but it is also persistent. A religious educator who wishes to realize a just world in the next year or two is in for disappointment and frustration. What a religious educator can do is take immediate steps to reduce the world's sufferings in a small but tangible way. The educator needs a certainty about the direction in which to go, combined with practical and realistic steps for starting on the journey. What follows, therefore, is a four-step method of religious education stated first in principles and then illustrated in the areas of work, family, food, and ecology.

Some people will probably find this approach not "radical" enough. They view the problem of social justice as one that demands passionate activity. I would readily agree on the need for political activity as a complement to the educational approach outlined here. If *radical* means getting to the root of a problem, then I think that religious education deserves a share of the word. Furthermore, I would claim that religious education ceases to be itself if it loses its contemplative outlook. The center of a religious educator's life has to be a peaceful and receptive attitude. Instead of lessening the time and energy available for social action, the peaceful center sustains the religious person in the face of insurmountable odds. Dorothy Day or Mother Teresa does not expect that her efforts will make the world just. What they do know from the center of their lives is that one cannot leave injustice as it is. The greater the injustice, the greater is the need for prayerful quiet in the midst of passionate activity.

This paradoxical union of contemplation and social action runs through the whole of Christian history. Meister Eckhart, a fourteenth-century Dominican, is generally regarded as the most outstanding example of Christian mysticism. My four-step pattern corresponds almost exactly to the fourfold path of spirituality in Eckhart as described by a modern commentator on his works.[1]

Closely related to the contemplative center and indispensable to religious education is a sense of humor. Much of the writing that advocates social justice is grimly serious. The movement that I describe in this chapter is a kind of playing at the limits, using paradoxical and even funny language. Is humor appropriate in a world where millions of children suffer and whole nations starve? The answer is that, like contemplation, humor becomes most important where injustice is greatest.

I am assuming, of course, that there are several kinds of humor. There is humor that trivializes important issues, and there is humor that is callously cruel to vulnerable people. But there is also a humor that sustains people in the midst of terrible suffering. In the previous chapter I described such humor as ironic and cited the Jewish experience as a dramatic example. The nature of this humor is incomprehensible to the solemnly serious who wish to get on with their plan to right the world. Religious humor arises from combining a vision of the universe's immensities with our passionate but small efforts in the middle of it all.

The Dilemma

By way of introduction to my four steps, I begin with the dilemma that confronts the religious educator who wishes to advocate a more just world. The dilemma is a real and a difficult one: How does any of us affirm the way the world should be, insisting upon that vision to our students, while at the same time remaining tolerant of other views and realistic about our limitations?

On the one side it is not enough to offer general principles about fairness, equality, and justice. Hardly anyone opposes abstract principles, and no one goes about advocating an unjust world. To use the concrete, poetic imagery of biblical and liturgical traditions is a big improvement. But it still needs translating or some kind of connecting into the hard political realities of today's institutions. On the other side, if any of us (even all of the leading scholars of the church) prepares a detailed plan for a just world, will it not be torn to pieces by disagreeing economists and unpredictable events?

What can religious educators do when faced with unimaginably complex issues that they can neither avoid nor solve? Most of us probably do one of two things: (1) Choose one issue which we think is the key to all issues. "Justice in this world begins with justice for _____." (2) Choose a guru whose statistics and strategies we trust. "Justice means following the direction advocated by _____." While both strategies can be useful, I think that they obscure the essential problem of a religious education. Both of them tend to turn education in religious matters into advocacy of a particular ideology. Liberation theories in church circles often combine a fundamentalist notion of revelation with some modern social theory.

Anything truly deserving the name *religious education* will be a peculiar and paradoxical combination. The two words do not go together comfortably. What is religious ties us to God beyond all the ordinary concerns of this world. In contrast, education engages us in dialogue with others so that we may find our place in this world. All education should presumably be concerned with a just world. What the qualifier *religious* does is to challenge our assumptions about what justice is and how to get there. Religious education moves toward a more just world by a peculiar kind of indirection and a strange-sounding language.

A Four-Step Solution

The process of religious education can be outlined in the following four steps:

1) The starting place is the gifts of life in any community. Community does not have to be invented although it may need shaping. We are all born into families, and we develop within networks of neighbors, friends, ethnic groupings, and work associates. Every community has a set of ordinary affairs, its rituals, codes, and daily tasks. Religious education depends for its beginning on the feeling of gratitude for the gifts of

ordinary life. Each morning is a miracle of grace: the sun, the air, the flowers, the food, and a thousand other gifts.

Any human being who reflects for a moment knows that humans did not invent the world nor are they in charge of the universe. The attitude of receptiveness to gifts is found in all children. If adults seem to lack this attitude, it is because they have forgotten what they once knew. I think that all of the great religions have this attitude at their center; certainly Jewish and Christian traditions do. "Give us this day our daily bread." "Give thanks to the Lord for all his gifts."

2) The ordinary in life is limited. We go through daily and habitual routines dimly conscious that there is more to life. Occasionally someone or some event jolts our awareness. Every person in the community is capable of recognizing that there are things which are out of the ordinary. Probably the most obvious example of the nonordinary is death.

Some people in a community are especially aware that ordinary life is merely ordinary. They do not repudiate the ordinary affairs of humans but they sense the limits of what most people most of the time take for granted. In particular, the ordinary distribution of the world's goods seems to be very unfair. The ordering of the ordinary world is not the only order there could be. The humans' share in arranging the way that things are is seriously flawed.

3) Religion teachers are those who have some vision of the nonordinary but who do not flee from the ordinary. They refuse to accept the limits of the ordinary world as the final limits of the universe. Far from hating the joys and pleasures of this world, they look for a way to deepen those joys and spread them to others.

The language for carrying out this process should be simple, poetic, and paradoxical. In the deeper appreciation of life's gifts and in the stories of a people's past, symbolic representations of a universal truth are found. One cannot completely convert the vision and its symbols into discursive statements. Great religious teachers play with language, often bending it back on itself in the form of double negatives. "I teach ill and the ending of ill," says the Buddha. Or in another formula: "Zen is the thorn for removing the thorn of our egos." Christian tradition is equally laden with negative words in both its doctrinal and ascetical histories. Terms which are negative in form (e.g., infinite) are often double negatives in meaning.

4) The claim made by a religious educator is neither "let's have a discussion in which all possibilities are open" nor "let me tell you the way things should be." Rather the claim is: "I and mine are not wrong; we have in our past and present an experience of something real and valuable. Join with us as we struggle against our biases and work to reduce the world's sufferings." A religion teacher tries to provide language, imagery, and practices to free people from illusion and strengthen their resistance to

evil. In destroying what destroys our community existence, we affirm a life together in justice and peace.

Humans never escape from limits. Even virtue must have its limits, as Montesquieu wisely noted. The great teacher pushes back the frontiers of our ordinary and unjust world only by imposing stronger discipline and new order. The task is liberation from specific oppressions; we must do nothing less, and we should attempt nothing more. We cannot create a better world than God's, and we should be hesitant to attribute what is wrong to God's intention. Our task is patiently and realistically to move in the right direction. In Thomas More's words: "What you can't put right you must try to make as little wrong as possible. For things will never be perfect until human beings are perfect—which I don't expect them to be for quite a number of years."[2]

Work

As my first illustration of an area that can embody these four steps I turn to work. In chapter 6 I described the struggle for a more adequate meaning of work as a central issue of religious education. There I stressed the danger of a reduction of work to employment, job, or occupation. Religious education is the maintaining of a tension between our ordinary job and our calling to accomplish God's work in this world.

Here I return to the same theme with a variation. A more ancient distinction than job and work is that between labor and work. Religious education for social justice has to include a fruitful tension between labor and work. The word *work* carries rich human meaning: the artist produces works, creation is the work of God.[3] In contrast, *labor* always refers to bodily exertion and to tasks which are never completed. We are born from a woman's labor and each day we (or someone for us) must continue the labors of the body.

Karl Marx is one who has taught the modern world that justice requires freeing masses of people from intolerable and oppressive burdens of labor. The struggle for justice is not just a Marxist project. But how does one bring about the change and, more important, where does the process lead? Much of modern philosophy, including Marxism, speaks of "man the worker" and posits some ideal beyond the limits of our bodily existence. The realm of freedom for them lies beyond the restrictions of oppressive labor. The approach of religious education would use a different language, imagery, and instruments. It would avoid sexism, activism, and the assumption of an ideal state attainable by human effort.

1) The first step is the recognition of irreducible human tasks: eating, clothing, care of the young, celebration, tending the sick, and so forth. A religious outlook, at least in Jewish and Christian traditions, views these tasks as burdensome but not evil. These daily tasks are often called "woman's work," but man's problem with work is related to an appreciation of labor. The monastic tradition in both Eastern and Western religion has always put a value upon "manual labor." Monastic reforms inevitably include a return to farming, household duties, and manual arts.

2) The second step is a recognition of the limits of labor and the limits of its arrangement. There is nothing very romantic about a "natural" condition in which many people starve to death. Labor simply gets us to the next day in the same way. Furthermore, the burdens are not equally distributed. The human race tends to divide on a sexual basis and also on class lines so that the tasks of labor become toils of drudgery. Religious education includes the recognition that God did not ordain one sex, one race, one class, or one nation to do "servile work."

3) Education involves striving to transcend the limits of physical labor with the creativity of human work. Discipline, imagination, and technology are needed if we are to fashion a better world. When we try to cut loose from the natural world, we do violence to it. Human works, as Luther taught, are not what saves us, and we cannot ultimately call any work our own. But we are called, nonetheless, to do our best in resisting oppression, thereby allowing the faith, grace, and works of God to be born within us. Daily labor is our reminder of finitude, but it is not an excuse for doing nothing about injustice.

4) The final step is the achieving of a better community, a world with less drudgery, suffering, and servility. We can reduce the amount of laborious effort and share the labor that remains. A compassion for all creatures great and small is what characterizes this last stage. As compassion, care, and a sense of connectedness with all of labor take root in our lives, then the last step becomes the first step for another cycle of human work at the edge of the present world.

This attitude to physical labor should be conveyed to children early in life. Religious education is the praise of human labor together with the reminder that God's works are greater than what human effort can accomplish. Still, humans are placed at the center of creation, called to respect the earth and transform it. The home is the chief training ground for understanding the necessity and dignity of labor. Later the school plays an important part by the way it speaks of work as well as by the curriculum.

Physical education and home economics are important to education in religious and moral matters. Girls were often excluded from competitive sports; boys similarly suffered from a deficiency in arts connected with the home.

When William James was asked what he would do to increase the ethical efficiency of the school, he answered: "I should increase enormously the amount of manual or 'motor' training relative to the book work, and not let the latter preponderate till the age of 15 or 16."[4] The battle for such a change was fought and lost in the second decade of this century. Today James's prescription is more important than ever, but people writing on moral development seem not to have the slightest awareness of it.

The economic system cannot be reformed unless boys and girls grow up with an appreciation of hard work, that is, physical toil, for the survival and improvement of human life. Until recently this proposal might have sounded anachronistic, but we are now entering the era of changed technology. The human tasks are still with us, needing to be taken care of with new forms of cooperation. The greater involvement of men in the care of home and children may be the most far-reaching revolution occurring in our time.

When one turns to international struggles for justice, the domestic lesson should not be lost. Economics is most often a choice between two evils. The poor cannot be left to starve in their rural isolation, but neither can the rich remove them from their physical environment with a guarantee of improvement. The work of the poor in impoverished lands has to be gradually improved mainly through the provision of basic education rather than by direct technical assistance.

Consultants from the rich world often have forgotten or else never learned the relation between physical labor and human work. Experts cannot create a new national economy by importing plans from other parts of the world. Advocates of social justice have to work patiently with the people, the land, and the market place which are already there. John K. Galbraith and Michael Harrington[5] agree that socialist planning has failed badly on this score. The poor countries are flooded with "administrators," but administrative skill is not easy to acquire. The mental ability to manage or administer has to grow organically from reflection on physical work in the setting of the home and the village.

Barbara Myerhoff's *Number Our Days* describes the people in a nursing home, among whom is a tailor named Schmuel. When asked why he continues to work hard, his reply is: "It is not the way of a Jew to make his work like there was no human being to suffer when it's done badly."[6] The double negative is strikingly evident here. Schmuel doesn't think that his work is going to make the world perfect. He starts from the realistic picture of a suffering world. He does his work the very best he can so as not to add to the world's woes. Religious education ought to cultivate this attitude of passionate involvement with the world's work and a gentle realism about the effects of our labor.

Family

Throughout U.S. history the family has been an object of obsessive concern. While it is assumed to be the one form of personal organization, it is also thought to be fragile and in danger of disintegrating. Various groups, including churches, are always rushing to the aid of the collapsing family. Some people assume that *parent education* is a contemporary invention, but since the seventeenth century parents have been subjected to an endless stream of advice from ministers, doctors, social workers, and self-appointed experts.

Church programs in family education today ought to question this cultural assumption. Family religious education may only add to the already available store of guides and gimmicks for parents. It may also support the impression that the family is the only form of personal life. The National Catechetical Directory calls the family the "church in miniature" and "a domestic church." These phrases are dangerously at odds with Catholic tradition that has always offered church participation in ways other than through the family. The real mission of family religious education is to affirm the family in relation to what is not the family.

The following description of family religious education is not just a repetition of what is everywhere accepted. By placing the topic of family into the context of justice, this sequence runs counter to programs that are almost exclusively psychological and interpersonal. Such programs are liable to reinforce the isolation of the family and its dependency on experts. Similarly, by situating the question of justice in the family, this sequence is in opposition to Lawrence Kohlberg's well-known stages of progress in moral reasoning. In Kohlberg's scheme the family is a hindrance to the perception of justice as social contract and categorical imperative.

1) The first step is recognition and acceptance of the family as inestimable gift. Nearly all of us are recipients of innumerable gifts from our families, a fact easily overlooked at a time when parents are blamed for whatever goes wrong. By *family* I mean the biological unit into which we are born, the ordinary world which we must both accept and transcend. Our seventeenth century Puritan ancestors praised the family, but they did not mean the "mere natural family." They wanted "a true Christian family"

in which each member would choose to belong to the Christian family which equaled church. Historian Michael Walzer wryly notes that Puritanism might have worked had the children kept arriving as immigrants instead of being born. Children are a powerful reminder of ordinary fleshly reality.[7]

For most of the human race the sense of the ordinary is established in early family experience. Before we accept a religious invitation to go beyond the ordinary, we need to prove that we can get that far. Parents usually remind us of our ordinary responsibilities at home and in school, to relatives and friends. The Hare Krishna and the Moonies of today are a continuation of seventeenth century Puritanism in promising the "true family." Their precondition is total disruption of ordinary family bonds, a tactic that usually produces false peace and abstract justice.

2) The family is limited. To spread the word *family* over every personal relation says both too little and too much. Such usage obscures the centrality of the parent-child relation in the meaning of family, and it also forces other relationships (sports team, law firm, school faculty, labor union, parish) into paternalistic forms. The family's limit is part of its strength. When we are young we need to feel secure and to know that the world is under control.

Numerous empirical studies now confirm what most parents probably sense: namely, that the parents' main educational function is to ward off excessive stimulation. Rationalistic educators who can only conceive education to be the informing of the mind and the expanding of consciousness completely misunderstood the family's educational role. A disadvantaged child is one who cannot get any buffer against the incessant noise of the street, the home, and the TV. The fortunate child is the one who can take in the world with the discipline and restraint provided by caring parents.[8]

3) The child who both knows what a family is and where the family ends has already begun to transcend the family. The individual family needs a context of other families and other kinds of groupings. A sense of neighborhood and a pride in ethnic roots are two ways in which the family is affirmed/transcended. When family life is weak, then clubs, associations, and friendships are seen to be competitive threats. But the family for its own health needs complementary structures into which family members can move.

The other way of affirming/transcending the family is to oppose elements in the environment that destroy the family. In this way the family is allowed its privacy, but aggressive action can be taken on its behalf. The Carnegie Council study *All Our Children*[9] directs attention away from psychological aids for parents to concern for tax restructuring, children's legal aid, family health services, and so on. A religious education that relates family and justice will strive to reduce the surrounding forces that harm the family.

4) The result of complementing the family and destroying its destroyers would be an enlarged sense of community and a redistribution of goods. We would not suddenly get equitable distribution of wealth, but we would be going in the right direction. We would be moving not toward a general principle of equality but toward a deepened sense of brother/sisterhood. We would recognize that sharing the wealth goes beyond monetary values; poor families often know something about human goods that rich people do not. Nonetheless, a sense of brother/sisterhood would lead to refusing to put up with intolerable evils. The warmth of family life is not a substitute for food and clothing.

The main challenge of family religious education is the existence of people who do not fit within the normal family. The test of justice, according to the Bible, is what you will do for a stranger. The poor, the lonely, the divorced, the widowed may not feel at home in church programs. The church must try to be a meeting ground where the family is supported and is at the same time challenged by the less fortunate of the world. Religious education is the maintaining of a tension between the simple, organic reality of the family and the vision of a united and just world.[10]

Food

Food is a special test of our attitude toward earthly possessions. Religious people should be keenly aware that in the end nothing belongs to humans. What we call our possessions are gifts for our proper use. "And to whom more is given, more will be expected in return." The Jewish Scriptures continually remind us that "the earth is the Lord's and the fullness thereof." Leviticus 25 and Deuteronomy 15 contain legislation for the years of release, the Sabbath years and the year of Jubilee. The clearing of human debts is founded on the single sentence: "The land shall not be sold in perpetuity for it is mine." Ironically, we constructed a doctrine of private property rights on the seventh commandment whose original meaning referred to the enslavement of other human beings.

Food is a special case because, as a fruit of the earth, it is like water or air: an absolute necessity which one group cannot rightly possess to excess while some people go starving. In the modern world, however, food is also a product of human technology and a part of the economic system.

While food cannot be separated from this latter context of a product, the scandal is that food is often a chief weapon in economic cartels and political conflicts.

The control of food is a dark secret unless we make an effort to understand the system and recognize our contribution to it. I think that every Christian today has an obligation to study U.S. policies on food. Barbara Ward has repeatedly made the point that for the first time in human history there is enough food to feed everyone, but up to two-thirds of the world is hungry. Part of the reason for this situation is: "Grain sheiks we can all become, using our appetites to rig the market."[11]

The greatest scandal lies in the sale and use of grain. Five multinational corporations control 85 percent of the trade. Most of these companies are located within the United States, but are under practically no controls. People are angry at the oil companies and want the U.S. government to do something. Unfortunately, the chief exploiters of the starving poor are not Exxon and Mobil but Cargill and Continental. These latter two names, largely unknown in this country, belong to the companies controlling 25 percent of the world's trade in grain. They are probably the two largest privately owned companies in the United States.[12]

1) The starting point in food education is appreciation for the extraordinary bounty in this country. The thing we are best at in the world is growing food. Iowa grows one-tenth of the world's corn; Kansas and South Dakota grow more wheat than Australia does. Toward this abundance of food people ought to have reverence. To prepare food well and to serve it with care are not obscene gestures in a starving world. We are an overfed and undernourished country. If we were to have more concern for the quality of food, we would probably use less and also be more sensitive to the needs of others.

2) We ought to recognize the limits of the present order. That we are overfed while most of the world is starving is not wholly explainable by our climate and our hard work. The international order is rigged to our advantage, and the problem continues to worsen. For example, South America has far more land to feed its people than the United States does, but it imports most of its food. Why? Because the most profitable thing is to cultivate coffee and sugar for sale in the United States. The problem may become even worse in Africa as the staple food of centuries is replaced by goods that are profitable to export to the rich countries.

3) The religious stance in this situation is to protest, by whatever legitimate means available, the unjust actions of rich governments (including our own) and agricultural monopolies. The first and absolute principle

is this: starvation is intolerable. Political advocacy has to be complemented by changes in personal modes of living. Catholics and Jews have traditionally seen dietary laws as central to religious life. We need new forms of fasting and abstaining that make ecological and economic sense today. Can we continue to feed 80 percent of our grain to cattle thereby losing 95 percent of the protein value by eating beef instead of grains? The rest of the world views our consumption of beef as a monstrous scandal.

4) The last step is a sharing of food with people who are in need and a celebration of that sharing in the Eucharist. The needy are not just in India or Cambodia but in old-age homes, lonely apartments, and in our neighborhoods. Sharing bread is the most basic of human gestures. We may forget that Jesus, in saying "man does not live on bread alone" (Matthew 4:14), was quoting Deuteronomy 8:3, which referred to those who are already well fed. Not on bread alone do we live but on bread and more than bread.

Through changing some of our personal habits and in sharing with the poor we can begin to reduce the terrible injustice of starvation. One of Gandhi's famous lines was: "There is enough for everyone's need, but not for everyone's greed." We don't think of ourselves as greedy, but we are part of an international order in which our country is a greedy partner. If we claim not to support that greed we have to advocate policies and live by habits that give evidence of resistance to greed. Education for justice in food allows nothing less.

Ecological Concerns

In this section I would like to use ecology as an illustration of the steps in an education for justice. Then as a summary statement I will use personal death and resurrection to illuminate the four steps. Kinship with all of God's creation is the route to realization of our own creaturehood. We are received bodily into God as we are enveloped in death by the earth.

What emerges in the course of the Hebrew Bible is the vision of a new and transformed earth. Micah provides the briefest summary of the accompanying ethic: "Do justly, love mercy, walk humbly with thy Lord." The New Testament confirms that vision and ethic, focusing upon Jesus of Nazareth as the beginning embodiment of a new earth and a new humanity.

We still live in the light of that vision. Even those people who reject the Jewish and Christian way cannot escape the continuing impact of the ideal of universal justice. Marxism, for example, with its chosen people and eschatological fulfillment is obviously derivative from Jewish and Christian history. Education for justice can mean nothing less than education and justice for all.

In recent decades one group after another has put forward its claim to justice. These days it is common to hear: "The issue is not black liberation, or women's liberation, but human liberation." This claim is in one way too general and in another way not general enough. Specific groups have historical problems for which specific remedies are needed. Human liberation can be an abstract idea manipulated by those in power. In the other direction, human liberation is still not broad enough to include care for all the nonhuman elements of the earth.

Justice on earth must include the earth and all its inhabitants. This view is not the romantic idea that each thing is of equal importance and that minerals, vegetables, and animals are not to serve the human. Humans were put on earth to name the animals and to tend the earth. However, the humans have no right to exploit the earth and to savage it at will. A nonviolent attitude to the less than human is a test of our attempt to bring justice for all people. Thus, feminism is inherently bound up with ecology and both are at root religious issues. "Our final mandate is to redeem our sister, the earth, from the bondage to destruction, recognizing her as our partner in the creation of the new world."[13]

1) If we are ever to come to terms with the ecological problem we must begin by appreciating the miracles of nature. We are recipients at birth of the sun, the plants, the oceans, and a system of renewal that no human mind can grasp. Human technology is also a marvel and a gift but it is only a reshaping of nature's energies. Humans do not invent anything, they can only receive and respond.

In a celebrated argument at the beginning of our nation, Jefferson and Paine argued against Edmund Burke that "the land belongs to the living." They thought it foolish and oppressive to suppose that the land belongs to the dead. What they did not seem able to imagine was the possibility that the land does not *belong* to any of us. As Native Americans might have taught them, the land belongs only to God.

2) Education ought to make us aware that despite our enormous inheritance we have been living beyond our means. We had already overstepped our limits before 1940, but the advent of the nuclear age was a jump in kind and not just degree. War has become totally absurd in its level of destructive possibility, and preparation for war is itself a financial disaster. We need to recover some sense of limits, and that requires an unequivocal no to modern warfare. In the 103,000 words of the Vatican II

documents, the word *condemn* is used only once, and it is in reference to war. Of course, the Second Lateran Council (A.D. 1139) also condemned war because the bow and the arbalest "had become too efficiently murderous." But this time we really *are* at the limit where the entire earth shudders at the possibility of one irrational act.

Nuclear energy is the by-product of the armaments race, and in the 1950s it seemed to be the happy, moral side of the picture. We should have been able to sense that it shared in the leap beyond all manageable limits of human order. As late as 1975 the famed Rasmussen report of the National Regulatory Commission declared it was "unlikely that an accident was overlooked which would significantly change the overall risk." Events of 1979, however, led millions of ordinary citizens to question whether experts who presumed themselves in control of nuclear power can be trusted. Rationalism, Chesterton once defined, is a peculiar form of insanity in which one has lost everything but one's mind.

3) A hard look at both our rich resources and our inability to live within our means can lead to only one conclusion: the need for struggle against our selfish, addictive way of life. The United States' use of oil and other energy is indefensibly profligate. No one can successfully imitate our standard of living, and it is dangerous that some countries are even trying to do so. All the discussion about producing more oil or more coal obscures the main question at stake: a radical reduction in our use of nonrenewable resources.

At the beginning of the 1970s *ecology* may have seemed a faddish term for some élite group to push. By the end of the decade it had become increasingly clear that the issue of ecology is human survival. In the next two decades the United States will either drastically shift its energy policies or it will unleash war and nuclear power in a desperate effort to feed its energy addiction. Could we still be happy if we used much less? We forget that in 1963 we were using only half the electricity we are using now. Was life only half as happy then?

4) Education in ecology must finally be an experience in sharing what we have. We can either let our greed for wealth run on without limit or we can start accepting that limits can be a good thing. At the beginning of this century William James made the strange and prophetic comment: "It is certain that the prevalent fear of poverty among the educated classes is the worst moral disease from which our civilization suffers."[14] Piling up more wealth does not alleviate any of our fears of poverty; more money to the wealthy has the same effect as salt water to the thirsty.

The discipline of limits is one taught by all the great religions and probably is not acquirable without some religious help. That is why ecology is unavoidably a religious question. We could learn some things from Native American religion about attitudes toward nature and use of resources. We could also learn from the minority groups among us who have found ways to live happily outside the dream of unlimited wealth. For example, Joseph Barton in *Peasants and Strangers* documents the success story of Slovaks in Cleveland who stay where they are rather than move up the real estate ladder.[15] Such groups have been ridiculed in the past by the culture's majority, but minorities who have little wealth may yet have to instruct the rest of us in how to live happily within limits. People might then choose "growth in things that really count rather than in things that are merely countable."[16]

Summary: Personal Death/Resurrection

1) What are given to each of us individually are all the gifts described in this chapter: work, family, food, energy. The first appropriate reaction is gratitude and a simple joy in being alive. What a marvelous thing to be not only a creature but the center of creation. Only through the human are all things mediated back to God.

2) The human joy in living is tempered by the realization that one has at most a few score years to live. Children and youth find it nearly impossible to grasp the meaning of that fact. They know, of course, that we die, but death is such a long way off that the fact of it enters little into daily experience. By the time one is middle-aged, life's movement seems to have so accelerated that the years pass by in a headlong rush toward death. By the time of old age most people have befriended death as one they would rather not see for a while but who is always with them. The only alternative for the old is that they become embittered by their implacable enemy, death.

3) The acceptance of mortality is not equivalent to accepting that life has no meaning beyond the few years of one's earthly life. The given limits of our experience are not the final limits of the universe. With the strange paradoxical movement that has been illustrated in all the preceding cases, the religious stance is to accept the limits and by that acceptance to transcend the limits. Thus, the Christian response to death is neither to pretend that death is good nor to claim that we are really spirits who don't die. Instead, it is in the receptiveness to all life that we push beyond the limits of our own death.

Here language inevitably fails because there is no way we could describe a life beyond life even if we had some vision of it. Religious language is in the form of a double negative which expresses our hopes by denying that the limits of our language are the limits of the universe. The Christian word *resurrection* makes its affirmation as a double denial: that Jesus was not abandoned by God his Father and that what we call death is the death of death. Karl Rahner says resurrection "only forbids in a negative sense the exclusion of particular elements" of the human in a final state.[17]

4) A life which is just and which looks toward justice for all is lived with a clear recognition that this is a dying/rising world. One's outlook is not split in two, but there is a tension of apparent opposites. I have to expend my energies in trying to make a just world while I also realize that when I have lived and died the world will not look much different. I can and should devote myself to the struggle for justice, but I and any number like me cannot right the world.

Only a religious outlook enables one to live with that demanding tension. An education for justice that is not a religious education for justice would eventually do violence to one's self or to the world's resources. We cannot now or in our lifetimes make the world just, but, while accepting our finitude, we can say an absolute no to intolerable and unnecessary suffering. We can in innumerable ways begin to reduce the world's sufferings but only if we are content to live as people and not as gods.

The struggle for justice is the refusal of a suffering people to lose their sense of humor and their eye for beauty in a world that needs passionate resistance to evil. Christianity and Judaism clearly distinguish between justice and equality. We are not called to be equal, but what justice demands is that we share one another's burdens. Religious education is a search for the ways to rejoice in the joys of this life and to bear with its sorrows. By refusing to accept what destroys our communities, we reach out a hand to all in the world who are in need.

Conclusion

This book has been a twentieth-century narrative, the story of the encounter between religion and education. Only in the twentieth century has this encounter become evident, and we are still at the beginning stage of a field and a profession called *religious education.* In religion's meeting with education two things are likely to occur: (1) a transformation of the religious group from within, resulting in changed institutions and in new methods for transmitting the religious life to the next generation; (2) a conversation with other religious groups that will eventually lead to increased tolerance and mutual understanding. From education's side, an appreciation of religion might lead to a recovery of forms of education that were pushed aside by the modern school. Education could then transcend some of the rationalistic bias which limits our conceptions of maturity, adulthood, and "the whole human being."

In a dialogue each partner has to speak at least twice. In fact, if something develops in those first two exchanges we would expect the conversation to continue indefinitely. "True understanding does not tire of interminable dialogue and 'vicious circles' because it trusts that imagination will eventually catch at least a glimpse of the always frightening light of truth."[1] The danger with religion and education is that dialogue never begins because one side assumes that the relation can be established by a single and simple prescription. The result is a premature synthesis that subverts or eliminates one of the parties.

The first self-conscious attempt to invent a field of religious education was flawed by this kind of naiveté. As I pointed out, Protestant leaders in the United States at the beginning of the twentieth century launched "the religious education movement." This movement assumed an easy compatibility of the "new education" and the religious life. Education was leading the way and religion would have to change its ways if it was ever to be up-to-date. In a lyrical declaration of victory at the turn of the century, A. D. Mayo wrote: "The absolute religion of Jesus Christ . . . has won the greatest victory in the acceptance of the new education by the American people as the last and best organization of the gospel of love for God and men, for the training of American childhood and youth for sovereign American citizenship."[2]

Reinhold Niebuhr's was the clear voice of warning in the second third of this century. He cautioned his Protestant brethren against the illusion in the promise of modern education.[3] The application of rational techniques will never socialize all human beings into living contentedly with one another. The not-so-likable categories of sin, suffering, and salvation were being avoided in the education that claimed to be religious. In retrospect it seems that Niebuhr's criticism was accurate. What was called religious education in that period was too often a secularized education with a religious veneer. But what is the alternative? Is it that education is not so important (which Niebuhr seemed to imply), or that education must become more profoundly religious? I think that the latter policy is the one that makes sense for Protestant churches and other religious bodies in the 1980s.

The Roman Catholic church throughout this century has been steeply invested in educational institutions. However, the full impact of modern education did not occur until the past two decades. The Catholic church was not a major participant in the religious education movement between 1900 and 1940, but it has had a tradition both of "teaching religion" in its schools and of wrestling with the philosophical foundations of religion. In earlier eras those issues were pursued in mostly parochial ways but in an ecumenical era these issues may take on new life within Catholicism. The liturgical and contemplative strands of the Catholic tradition can also be of importance in the dialogue of religion and education.

Catholic and Protestant churches need the partnership of Judaism or the tension between *religious* and *Christian* is likely to disappear. Jews are still struggling with the place of modern education, although in some respects Jews preceded Christians in this encounter. Judaism was forced into an alliance with secular enlightenment as a way of escaping Christian domination. In the last two centuries, Jews have been through several phases of outdoing the secularists at their own game and of protecting Jewish life from all intrusions. The United States is the obvious place for a Christian-Jewish dialogue that might change the self-image of both parties. Such a dialogue would be the clearest single sign today that religious education is emerging.

The other group that deserves comment here is Islam. Nowhere is the conflict of modern education and traditional religion more acute than in the Muslim world. Until 1955 most books on Muslim education were written by Western Christian scholars.[4] As one might guess, there was considerable bias in the writings of a group that considered itself superior. In the last quarter century Islam has begun taking hold of its own destiny, including its own educational system. The attitude toward Western values in education has been one of extreme reaction, and that trend is likely to grow in this decade. Islam is interested in Islamic education, not in a dialectic of religion and education. "The primary purpose of education should be to imbue students with their religion and ideology. . . . Education should produce men with deeply held convictions about the Islamic ideals of individual and collective life."[5]

Islam thus represents the most difficult test case of a religious education. Christians and Jews may misunderstand each other, but both groups believe that understanding is desirable and that, at least to a degree, understanding is possible. But Muslims at this time profess not to want a study or an understanding of their religion by outsiders. Given the last two centuries of Christian-Muslim relations, their distrust is not surprising. Despite the apparent absence of dialogue that would include Muslims in religious education, two points should be noted: (1) Dialogue is not restricted to rational discourse or even to words. When there has been distrust between two parties, polite and discursive speech has to be preceded by other forms of exchange. Boycotts or marches are a common form of beginning. Even hostage-taking is a form of communication, a plea for recognition. (2) Respect for the integrity of the others with whom one is trying to communicate entails allowing them to break off communication if they choose to do so. It also allows one to argue that they *should not* break off communication, even though they have a right to do so.[6]

The dialogue which would produce a field and a profession of religious education could be diagrammed this way:

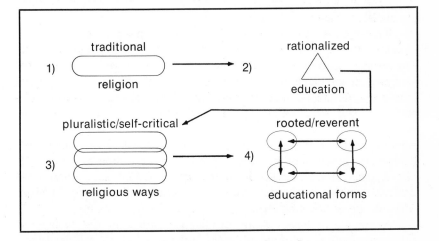

In this pattern the religious beginning is a simple "God and my people." As religion is forced to reflect on itself and to see its own limits, other ways of being religious come into view. The rational criticism from modern education can be experienced as a threat to the very existence of a religious way. But if there is truly a people with a life of ritual and a contemplative center, the criticism can give new meaning to religion. If it is God in whom we trust then why become defensive about the doctrines and precepts of our people? Why not rejoice that God's gifts go beyond the limits of our people and our imaginations?

David Steindl-Rast pinpoints the division in religion today as "between those whose religious commitment is inclusive because they give themselves to the truth, and those whose religious commitment is exclusive, because they think of truth as something of which one takes possession."[7] Where the attitude is inclusive, then education is not only allowed but welcomed. A religious outlook may be wary of claiming to include too much too soon. Nonetheless, a self-critical religiousness is intent on living whatever truth is within our experience and leaving to God the final judgment about who "possesses" the most truth.

The educational change that is implied by the above diagram is as drastic as the religious change. Modern education tends to be housed in one kind of institution and to use one set of instruments. If education truly encounters religion (as opposed to tucking it into the school curriculum), education would take on a diversity of forms with qualities I have called *rooted* and *reverent*. Education would have roots in the earth, the body, and the family. Without diminishing its drive toward rational inquiry, education can be reconceptualized to include community life, daily work, and contemplative quiet. Education would be centered on how people are living and would be concerned with improving the main forms in which people learn the art of living.

If a self-critical/pluralistic religiousness could meet a rooted/reverent education then there would emerge a complex field of religious education. The result would be a large and sprawling project. However, it would not be a vaguely defined area or a set of generalities. Religious education would include the discipline, direction, and instruction that enable us to understand our own religious history and to live by its best lights. Religious education in the twentieth century also includes reaching some understanding of other religious groups. Religious education can neither be different from education nor a minor branch of education. It has to be a concern that shows up at various points throughout education, and most obviously it has to be a constant reminder that education is never finished while we are earthly creatures.

As for the professionalizing of religious education, the twenty-first century may see a postmodern form of professional which includes all the needed elements. For now, as I have described in chapter 7, there are two professions which should exist in fruitful tension. Stated in Christian terms, the relation is between "church minister in education" and "modern educator in religion." The first has its base in the religious institution, the second is defined by its educational base. The slow movement and the complex operation of big institutions prevent any quick synthesis of these two professions. From the religious (here, the church) side, we need minister and ministry reaching out to education both for serving people in need and for transforming the very meaning of education. From the educational side we need critical tools within ecclesiastical settings to provoke thinking and to challenge institutional forms, including everything being called "ministry" today.

The last four chapters of this book have been an attempt to show implications for a field and a profession of religious education. What do *adult education, moral development, adult development,* and *education for justice* mean? I think that the answers assumed today are prematurely taken from either religion or education. A dialogue between religion and education would make us question whether we know where we are going and whether we are sure of the steps to get there. Educational specialists are likely to be interested in getting the aim clearly stated and then devising a sequence that takes us straight to the end. If modern education adverts to religion at all in these matters, it will probably be to invoke the increased motivation that religion might supply, especially on matters of morality.

Religion does not contradict the educational aims of maturity, development, adulthood, justice, and so on, but it does raise the question of human fallibility on all these issues. No human being is the final judge of success. Whatever the differences of Christians, Jews, and Muslims, all of them insist upon the proposition: "Justice is mine, says the Lord." If religion is not allowed into the description of adulthood or justice, then education will be culturally biased in whom it educates and to what it educates. Religion does not contradict a rational sequence toward educational goals, but it reminds us that community life, daily work, and moments of quiet are also steps along the way. The religious path has a lot of cycles if not circles built into it. One of its chief characteristics is playfulness, an element that should not be excluded from descriptions of adulthood, moral development, or justice.

A main key to the meaning of religious education, and the element perhaps most alien to modern education, is what I have called *recollective wisdom* or *contemplative leisure.* I do not equate this element with prayer, although it is closely related to a form of prayer. It would be undesirable if not blasphemous to make prayer an instrument of education. Prayer is simply prayer, an act directed toward God. But the attitude which is found in prayer lies also at the base of contemplative leisure so that the possibility and the context of prayer can be a test of all education.

The listening for the divine and the recognition that we are not the final measure of things are the marks of a religious education.

This attitude of receptivity and humility is difficult to maintain in struggles for human liberation. For example, Robert Heilbroner, writing both in praise and criticism of Marxism, notes: "The laudable element in Marxism is its declaration that the only 'meaning' to be ascribed to history is its moral unfolding, or more precisely, its orientation to human freedom."[8] The orientation to human freedom may indeed be laudable. Nevertheless, one must ask whether the meaning of history is reducible to "moral unfolding," that is, whether relentlessly pursuing the moral end that has been declared the only meaning to history is healthy for human beings, not to mention nonhuman creatures.

An alternative approach to the struggle for justice has deep roots in Christian tradition. Thomas Merton and Daniel Berrigan in the contemporary period are in a long line that goes back to Ruysbroeck and Eckhart in the Middle Ages. The contemplative or mystical attitude grounds the passionate protest for social justice. Meister Eckhart is probably the outstanding example of mysticism in Christian tradition, but he has not often been seen in this context of social justice. Seldom quoted is his line: "He who understands my teaching about justice and the just person understands everything I say."[9] He was condemned by the Inquisition for confusing the unlearned people and, while he may have done some of that, he also seems to have stirred up some of those poor and unlearned people, giving them a new vision of themselves and the social order. A contemporary Marxist acknowledges of Eckhart: "A subject who thought himself to be in personal union with the Lord of Lords provided . . . a very poor example indeed of serfhood."[10]

Our world badly needs the passion and vision of religion tempered by the forms and rationality of education. Religious emotion runs high around the world, much as it did in Eckhart's fourteenth century. If the outlets for this force are not political and educational, then the result is bound to be violence. The construction of the channels of expression is so large a project that none of us can do more than make a small contribution. But the large religious organizations ought to be recognizing the need for a religious education whose requirements far transcend the attention, effort, and money so far committed to the venture. Religious education is an idea whose time has arrived.

Notes

CHAPTER ONE

1. David Hall, *The Faithful Shepherd: A History of the New England Ministry in the 17th Century* (Chapel Hill: University of North Carolina, 1972), p. 156.

2. The line is from Horace Bushnell's *Christian Nurture*, but even the most liberal of Christian religious educators, George Albert Coe, could make it his own in "Religious Education as a Part of General Education," *Who Are We?*, ed. John Westerhoff (Birmingham: Religious Education Press, 1978), p. 22.

3. Didier-Jacques Piveteau and J. T. Dillon, *Resurgence of Religious Instruction* (Notre Dame: Religious Education Press, 1977).

4. Ibid., pp. 173-74.

5. Joseph Featherstone, "Family Matters," in *Harvard Educational Review* 49 (February, 1979), p. 35.

6. For the history of this cycle, see Eva Brann, *Paradoxes of Education in a Republic* (Chicago: University of Chicago, 1979).

7. John Dewey, *Democracy and Education* (New York: Free Press, 1966), p. 4.

8. For an interesting example of change at the end of the 1970s, see Neil Postman, *Teaching as a Conservative Activity* (New York: Delacorte, 1979).

9. Most Protestants have forgotten or are unaware that *catechetics* was once a Protestant language too. For example, see Cotton Mather, *Magnalia Christi Americana* (New York: Frederick Ungar, 1970), referring to the catechizing of the New England divines (p. 101) and John Cotton as the catechist of Emmanuel College (p. 67).

10. Wilfred Paradis, "Catechesis in the Catholic Community," in *Religious Education* 74 (January/February, 1979), p. 50.

CHAPTER TWO

1. George A. Coe, "What Is 'Religious' Education?" in *Who Are We?*, ed. John Westerhoff (Birmingham: Religious Education Press, 1978), p. 56.

2. See Harrison Elliot, *Can Religious Education Be Christian?* (New York: Macmillan, 1940), pp. 1-12.

3. For the religious significance of the difference between United States and America, see Gabriel Moran, "Religious Education Toward America," in *Religious Education* 72 (September/October, 1977), pp. 473-83.

4. George A. Coe, "Religious Education as a Part of General Education," in *Who Are We?,* p. 20.

5. Quoted in Everett Carter, *The American Idea* (Durham: University of North Carolina, 1977), p. 196.

6. Mary Wollstonecraft, *A Vindication of the Rights of Woman,* ed. Charles Hagelman, Jr. (New York: Norton, 1967), p. 233.

7. Nevin Harner, "Is Religious Education to Become a Science?" in *Who Are We?,* p. 87.

8. A. C. McGiffert (1917) quoted in H. Shelton Smith, *Faith and Nurture* (New York: Scribner, 1941), p. 53.

9. William C. Bower, *The Curriculum of Religious Education* (New York: Scribner, 1925), p. 20.

10. George A. Coe, *What Is Christian Education?* (New York: Scribner, 1929), p. 29.

11. See Bower, op. cit., p. 67.

12. See George A. Coe, *A Social Theory of Religious Education* (New York: Scribner, 1917), pp. 15f.

13. George Santayana, *Winds of Doctrine* (New York: Scribner, 1926), p. 191.

14. John Dewey, "Religion and Our Schools," in *Characters and Events,* ed. Joseph Ratner (New York: Henry Holt, 1929), II, p. 512.

15. Mildred Newman and Bernard Berkowitz, *How to Be Your Own Best Friend* (New York: Ballantine, 1974), p. 53.

16. F. Ernest Johnson, *The Social Gospel Re-examined* (New York: Harper and Brothers, 1940), pp. 71f.

17. Dewey, op. cit., p. 512.

18. Ernest J. Chave, *A Functional Approach to Religious Education* (Chicago: University of Chicago, 1947), p. 97.

19. W. Evans Powell, *Education for Life with God* (New York: Abingdon, 1934).

20. James Smart, *The Teaching Ministry of the Church* (Philadelphia: Westminster, 1954), p. 59.

21. Smith, *Faith and Nurture,* chapters 2, 3, 4.

CHAPTER THREE

1. Philip Wheelwright, *The Burning Fountain,* 2nd ed. (Bloomington: Indiana University, 1968), pp. 3-17.

2. Gabriel Moran, *Design for Religion* (New York: Herder and Herder, 1970), chapter 1.

3. Lawrence Cremin, *Public Education* (New York: Basic Books, 1976), p. 27.

4. Charles Silberman, *Crisis in the Classroom* (New York: Random House, 1970).

5. See R. S. Peters, *Education and the Education of Teachers* (Boston: Routledge and Kegan Paul, 1977), pp. 3-21.

6. Arnold Toynbee, "What Should Be the Christian Approach to the Contemporary Non-Christian Faiths?" in *Attitudes Toward Other Religions,* ed. Owen Thomas (London: 1969), pp. 160f.

7. Lewis Thomas, *The Medusa and the Snail* (New York: Viking, 1979), p. 2.

8. Erik Erikson, *Young Man Luther* (New York: Norton, 1958), p. 67.

9. Deane William Ferm, " 'The Road Ahead in Theology' Revisited," *Christian Century,* May 9, 1979, p. 527.

10. Edmund Burke, *Reflections on the Revolution in France* (New York: Holt, Rinehart and Winston, 1962), p. 111.

11. Hans Gadamer, *Truth and Method* (New York: Seabury, 1975), pp. 239f.

CHAPTER FOUR

1. See Carl Henry, *God, Revelation and Authority,* Vol. I (Waco, Texas: Word, Inc., 1977). Of exceptions to my generalization I should note Avery Dulles, "The Symbolic Structure of Revelation," *Theological Studies* 41 (March, 1980), pp. 51-73; Richard McBrien, *Catholicism* (New York: Winston, 1980), pp. 201-43.

2. At the end of W. Cantwell Smith's detailed study of faith, he acknowledges the need for a study of revelation and also admits that no such study exists; *Faith and Belief* (Princeton: Princeton University, 1979), p. 169.

3. James Hillman, "Peaks and Vales," in *On the Way to Self Knowledge,* eds. Jacob Needleman and Dennis Lewis (New York: Knopf, 1976), p. 128.

4. Bernard Weisberger, *They Gathered at the River* (Boston: Little, Brown and Co., 1958), p. 95.

5. Norman Vincent Peale, *The Power of Positive Thinking* (Old Tappan, N.J.: Fleming H. Revell Co., 1956), p. 181.

6. See Morton White, *Science and Sentiment in America* (New York: Oxford, 1972), p. 25.

7. See Richard Hofstadter, *Anti-Intellectualism in America* (New York: Vintage, 1963), p. 122.

8. See John Dominic Crossan, *Raid on the Articulate* (New York: Harper and Row, 1976).

CHAPTER FIVE

1. F. Ernest Johnson, *The Social Gospel Re-examined* (New York: Harper and Brothers, 1940), p. 188.

2. See American Council on Education, Committee on Religion and Education, *The Relation of Religion to Public Education: The Basic Issues,* ser. 1, Report of Committees and Conferences 11 (Washington, 1947).

3. See Sheila Rothman, *Woman's Proper Place* (New York: Basic, 1978), p. 57.

4. See Redding Sugg, *Motherteacher: The Femininization of American Education* (Charlottesville: University of Virginia, 1978).

5. Horace Bushnell, *Christian Nurture* (New Haven: Yale, 1967).

6. Kenneth Eble, *Professors as Teachers* (San Francisco: Jossey-Bass, 1973).

7. Kenneth Eble, *The Craft of Teaching* (San Francisco: Jossey-Bass, 1978), p. 42.

8. Ian Barbour, *Myths, Models and Paradigms* (New York: Harper and Row, 1974), p. 134.

9. See Philip Phenix, "Religion in Public Education: Principles and Issues," in *Religion in Public Education,* ed. David Engel (New York: Paulist, 1974), p. 67.

10. Edward Robinson, *The Original Vision* (Oxford: Manchester College, 1977), chapter 6.

11. James Smart, *The Teaching Ministry of the Church* (Philadelphia: Westminster, 1954), pp. 59-60.

12. Ibid., p. 131.

13. Jean Holm, *Teaching Religion in School* (London: Oxford, 1975), p. 5.

CHAPTER SIX

1. See Joseph O'Toole, *Work and the Quality of Life* (Cambridge: MIT Press, 1974).

2. John Calvin, *Institutes,* ed. J. T. McNeill, Library of Christian Classics (London: Oxford University, 1960), p. 725.

3. Quoted in Norman O. Brown, *Life Against Death* (Middletown: Wesleyan, 1959), p. 36.

4. Thomas Green, *Work, Leisure and American Schools* (New York: Random House, 1968), p. 16.

5. See Louise Kapp Howe, *Pink Collar Workers* (New York: Putnam, 1977), pp. 246-48.

6. Sebastian de Grazia, *Of Time, Work and Leisure* (New York: Twentieth Century Fund, 1962), p. 203.

7. John Garraty, *Unemployment in History* (New York: Harper and Row, 1978), p. 4.

8. John Dewey, *Democracy and Education* (New York: Free Press, 1966), chapter 23.

9. Abraham Heschel, *The Sabbath* (New York: Farrar, Straus and Giroux, 1975), p. 76.

CHAPTER SEVEN

1. The title of an excellent article by Harold Wilensky in *American Journal of Sociology* 70 (September, 1964), pp. 137-158.

2. See Burton Bledstein, *The Culture of Professionalism* (New York: Norton, 1976); Daniel Calhoun, *Professional Lives in America* (Cambridge: Harvard, 1965); David Hall, *The Faithful Shepherd* (Chapel Hill: University of North Carolina, 1972); Thomas Haskell, *The Emergence of Professional Social Science* (Urbana: University of Illinois, 1977); Paul Mattingly, *The Classless Profession* (New York: New York University, 1977); Donald Scott, *From Office to Profession* (Philadelphia: University of Pennsylvania, 1978).

3. For the strengths and limitations of DRE, see Maria Harris, "The Future of the Profession from a Catholic Perspective," *Parish Religious Education* (New York: Paulist, 1978), pp. 217-231; Maria Harris, *The DRE Book* (New York: Paulist, 1976); and *The DRE Reader* (Winona, MN: Saint Mary's Press, 1980), edited by Maria Harris.

4. Washington, United States Catholic Conference, 1978.

5. See Robert Jay Lifton, *The Life of the Self* (New York: Simon and Schuster, 1976), pp. 165f.

6. See Daniel Boorstin, *The Americans: The Colonial Experience* (New York: Random House, 1958), pp. 185-239.

7. See Arthur Wirth, *Education in the Technological Society* (San Francisco: Intext, 1972), p. 6.

8. Christopher Lasch's much publicized book, *The Culture of Narcissism* (New York: Norton, 1979), is an assault on this pattern of professional/consumer. Unfortunately, Lasch makes no attempt to describe an alternative pattern except to say in the next to last paragraph of the book that we need "communities of competence."

9. Dorothy Jean Furnish, *DRE/DCE: The History of a Profession* (Nashville: United Methodist, 1976).

10. Jethro Lieberman, *Crisis at the Bar* (New York: Norton, 1978); esp. p. 223.

11. Ibid., p. 106.

CHAPTER EIGHT

1. *Catechesis of Revelation* (New York: Herder and Herder, 1966).

2. Orestes Brownson, as quoted in Richard de Lone, *Small Futures* (New York: Harcourt, Brace, Jovanovich, 1979), p. 44.

3. Horace Bushnell, *Christian Nurture* (New Haven: Yale, 1967), p. 66.

4. For more details of this history, see my *Education Toward Adulthood* (New York: Paulist, 1979), chapter 1.

5. As the distinction is made by Walter Perry; see "Locked into an Outdated Philosophy of Learning," *The Chronicle of Higher Education,* November 27, 1978.

6. See *Lifelong Learning and Public Policy* (Washington: HEW, 1978).

7. See Darrett Rutman, *Winthrop's Boston* (Chapel Hill: University of North Carolina, 1965), p. 258.

8. Ashley Montagu, "Don't Be Adultish," *Psychology Today,* August, 1977, pp. 46f.

9. John Dewey, *Reconstruction in Philosophy* (Boston: Beacon, 1957), p. 185.

10. Paul Ripple in *The Parish in Community and Ministry,* eds. Evelyn Eaton Whitehead and James D. Whitehead, (Notre Dame: University of Notre Dame, 1978), p. 25.

11. Leon McKenzie, *Adult Education and the Burden of the Future* (Washington: University Press of America, 1979), pp. 64, 61, 92.

12. On the "Meanings of Adult" see my *Education Toward Adulthood,* chapter 2.

13. See Evelyn Eaton Whitehead and James D. Whitehead, *Christian Life Patterns* (Garden City: Doubleday, 1979), pp. 37f.

CHAPTER NINE

1. Lawrence Kohlberg, "Moral Development, Religious Education and the Public Schools: A Developmental View," in *Religion and Public Education,* ed. Theodore Sizer (Boston: Houghton and Mifflin, 1967), pp. 164-83.

2. For criticism, see William Kurtines and Esther Blank Greif, "The Development of Moral Thought: Review and Evaluation of Kohlberg's Approach," in *Psychological Bulletin* 81 (August, 1974), pp. 453-70.

3. See Lawrence Kohlberg, "Moral Education Reappraised," in *The Humanist* 38 (November, 1978), pp. 13-15.

4. Carol Gilligan, "In a Different Voice: Women's Conception of the Self and Morality," in *Harvard Educational Review* 47 (November, 1977), pp. 481-517; "Woman's Place in Man's Life Cycle," in *Harvard Educational Review* 49 (November, 1979), pp. 431-46.

5. (New York: Harcourt, Brace and Co., 1932).

6. See Jean Piaget and Barbel Inhelder, *The Psychology of the Child* (New York: Basic, 1969); Brian Rotman, *Jean Piaget: Psychologist of the Real* (Ithaca: Cornell, 1977), p. 21.

7. David Elkind, *Children and Adolescents* (New York: Oxford, 1970), p. 83.

8. Piaget, *Moral Judgment of the Child,* p. 13.

9. Elkind, op. cit., p. 12

10. Piaget, *Moral Judgment of the Child,* p. 191.

11. Ibid., p. 405.

12. Ibid., p. 323.

13. Quoted in Howard Muson, "Moral Thinking: Can It Be Taught?" in *Psychology Today,* February, 1979, p. 54.

14. See Kohlberg, *Religion and Public Education;* "Education for Justice," in *Moral Education* (Cambridge: Harvard, 1970), pp. 57-83.

15. Kohlberg, *Religion and Public Education,* p. 170; see also E. L. Simpson, "Moral Development Research: A Case Study of Scientific Cultural Bias," in *Human Development* 17 (1974), pp. 81-106.

16. Kohlberg, *Religion and Public Education,* p. 173.

17. See note 4 above.

18. Gilligan, "In a Different Voice," p. 498.

19. Ibid., p. 507.

20. Ibid., p. 513.

21. See Muson, op. cit., p. 51.

22. Kohlberg, "Moral Education Reappraised," pp. 13-15.

23. Erik Erikson, *Childhood and Society,* 2nd ed. (New York: Norton, Dutton, 1976), pp. 247-74.

24. For an example, see Gail Sheehy, *Passages* (New York: Dutton, 1976).

CHAPTER TEN

1. See George Vaillant, *Adaptation to Life* (Boston: Little, Brown and Co., 1977).

2. Daniel Levinson, *The Seasons of a Man's Life* (New York: Knopf, 1978), p. 199.

3. Marjorie Fiske Lowenthal, *Four Stages of Life* (San Francisco: Jossey-Bass, 1976), pp. 220, 235.

4. Studs Terkel, *Working* (New York: Pantheon, 1972), p. xviii.

5. Levinson, op. cit., p. 217.

6. John Murray Cuddihy, *No Offense* (New York: Seabury, 1978), p. 187.

7. Martin Buber, *Eclipse of God* (New York: Harper, 1960), pp. 34f.

8. Mircea Eliade, *The Sacred and the Profane* (New York: Harper, 1959).

9. Woody Allen, *Without Feathers* (New York: Random House, 1975), p. 194.

10. Albert Camus, quoted in John Dominic Crossan, *Raid on the Articulate* (New York: Harper and Row, 1976), p. 94.

11. See Crossan, op. cit.

12. Harry Levinson, *Executive Stress* (New York: Harper and Row, 1964), p. 278.

13. Geoffrey Gorer, *Death, Grief and Mourning* (Garden City: Doubleday, 1965), p. 121.

14. See the summary of literature on the subject in: Ibid., pp. 136-52.

15. Erik Erikson, *Insight and Responsibility* (New York: Norton, 1964), p. 134.

16. Levinson, *The Seasons of a Man's Life,* p. 335.

CHAPTER ELEVEN

1. See Matthew Fox, "Meister Eckhart's Spiritual Journey," in *Western Spirituality,* ed. Matthew Fox (Notre Dame: Fides, 1979), pp. 215-248.

2. Thomas More, *Utopia* (Baltimore: Penguin, 1965), p. 64.

3. In the Hebrew Bible, see especially the Psalms (104:24; 105:5; 107:23-24; 111:2-6); in the New Testament, see especially John's Gospel (5:17; 17:14).

4. Quoted in M. Sadler, *Moral Instruction and Training in the School* (New York: Holt, 1908), p. 94.

5. John Kenneth Galbraith, *The Nature of Mass Poverty* (Cambridge: Harvard, 1979); Michael Harrington, *The Vast Majority* (New York: 1978).

6. Barbara Myerhoff, *Number Our Days* (New York: Dutton, 1979), p. 172.

7. Michael Walzer, *The Revolution of the Saints* (Cambridge: Harvard, 1965), p. 196.

8. See Rudolph Schafer, *Mothering* (Cambridge: Harvard, 1977); Janet Bennet, "Parents Are 'The People' Too!" in Alfred McBride, *Creative Teaching in Christian Education* (Boston: Allyn and Bacon, 1979), pp. 199-251.

9. Kenneth Keniston, *All Our Children* (New York: Harcourt, 1977).

10. See Gabriel Moran, "The Way We Are: Communal Forms and Church Response," in *Parish Religious Education,* ed. Maria Harris (New York: Paulist, 1978), pp. 25-40.

11. Barbara Ward, *The Home of Man* (New York: Norton, 1976), p. 279.

12. Dan Morgan, *Merchants of Grain* (New York: Viking, 1979).

13. Rosemary Radford Ruether, *New Woman, New Earth* (New York: Seabury, 1975), p. 83.

14. William James, *The Varieties of Religious Experience* (New York: New American Library, 1958), p. 285.

15. Joseph Barton, *Peasants and Strangers* (Cambridge: Harvard, 1975).

16. Amory Lovins, *Soft Energy Paths* (New York: Harper, 1979), p. 57.

17. Karl Rahner, *Foundations of Christianity* (New York: Seabury, 1978), p. 269.

CONCLUSION

1. Hannah Arendt, "Understanding and Politics," *Partisan Review* 20 (July/August, 1953), p. 392.

2. A. D. Mayo, "The New Education—The Christian Education," *Education* 19 (May, 1897), p. 312.

3. See *Moral Man and Immoral Society* (New York: Scribner, 1932) with a new introduction in 1960 reaffirming his position.

4. See G. H. Jansen, *Militant Islam* (New York: Harper, 1979), pp. 75f.

5. Khurshid Ahmad, *Principles of Islamic Education* (Lahore: United, 1968), p. 10.

6. Robert Neville, *Soldier, Sage, Saint* (New York: Fordham, 1978), p. 15.

7. See Donald Dawe and John Carman, eds., *Christian Faith in a Religiously Plural World* (New York: Orbis, 1978), p. 134.

8. Robert Heilbroner, *Marxism For and Against* (New York: Norton, 1980), p. 80.

9. Matthew Fox, "Meister Eckhart and Karl Marx: The Mystic as Political Theologian," *Understanding Mysticism,* ed. Richard Woods (Garden City: Image, 1980), p. 545.

10. Ibid., p. 552.